the Weekend Crafter®

Marbling

the Weekend Crafter®

Marbling

Easy & Elegant Projects for Paper & Fabric

LAURA SIMS

LARK
BOOKS

A Division of Sterling Publishing Company, Inc.
New York

THIS BOOK IS DEDICATED
TO MY MOTHER, SARAH P. SIMS,
A GRACIOUS WOMAN.

Acknowledgments

I would especially like to thank the craft artists who participated in the gallery. They each shared their time and creative energy to incorporate marbling into their own specialties for this book.

Many thanks to Mike Townshend in the Research and Development department of Golden Paint Company, a former marbler and valuable source for technical information.

Also, I want to thank Joanne O'Sullivan, my editor, for her enthusiasm and calm encouragement, and Evan Bracken, for his good humor and versatile skills in "telling a story" with photography.

Lastly, I want to thank my husband, Jim Charneski, for his constant support.

EDITOR:
JOANNE O'SULLIVAN

ART DIRECTOR & PRODUCTION:
SUSAN MCBRIDE

COVER DESIGN:
BARABARA ZARETSKY

PHOTOGRAPHY:
EVAN BRACKEN

ILLUSTRATIONS:
ORRIN LUNDGREN

EDITORIAL ASSISTANCE:
ANNE WOLFF HOLLYFIELD

PRODUCTION ASSISTANCE:
HANNES CHAREN

PROOFREADER:
KIM CATANZARITE

Library of Congress Cataloging-in-Publication Data

Sims, Laura.
    Marbling : easy & elegant projects for paper & fabric / Laura Sims.
        p.cm.—(The weekend crafter)
    Includes index.
    ISBN 1-57990-195-6 (pbk.)
    1. Marbling. 2. Textile painting. I. Title II. Series.

TT385 .S495 2002
745.7—dc21

10 9 8 7 6 5 4 3 2

Published by Lark Books, a division of
Sterling Publishing Co., Inc.
387 Park Avenue South, New York, N.Y. 10016

© 2002, Laura Sims

Distributed in Canada by Sterling Publishing,
c/o Canadian Manda Group, One Atlantic Ave., Suite 105
Toronto, Ontario, Canada M6K 3E7

Distributed in the U.K. by Guild of Master Craftsman Publications Ltd.,
Castle Place, 166 High Street, Lewes, East Sussex,
England
BN7 1XU
Tel: (+ 44) 1273 477374, Fax: (+ 44) 1273 478606, Email: pubs@thegmcgroup.com,
Web: www.gmcpublications.com

Distributed in Australia by Capricorn Link (Australia) Pty Ltd.,
P.O. Box 704, South Windsor NSW 2756, Australia

If you have questions or comments about this book, please contact:
Lark Books
67 Broadway
Asheville, NC 28801
(828) 236-9730

Printed in China

ISBN 1-57990-195-6

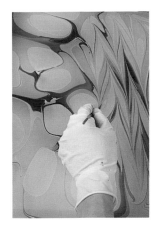

CONTENTS

INTRODUCTION

CAUTION: MARBLING IS MAGIC. You may think that you're playing for a weekend, only to discover that you're hooked for a lifetime.

Marbling cast its spell on me in 1985. While working at John C. Campbell Folk School in Brasstown, North Carolina, I received an invitation to travel with my friend Nancy Lawrence to Seattle, Washington, to visit her daughter and see the sights. Before leaving North Carolina, Nancy had taken a marbling class with a well-known marbler, Patty Schleicher, and was totally mesmerized by the process.

As we drove across the country, the changing landscapes and variegated skies that we saw constantly reminded Nancy of the swirls of colors and patterns of marbling. One evening, I even woke to hear her excitedly talking about colors in her sleep.

Upon reaching our destination, we visited Colophon Book Arts, a source for marbling supplies. We entered the basement studio of the proprietor, Don Guyot, to find shelves of paints, supplies, and samples of marbling. As fate would have it, there was an upcoming class at the studio, but only one space remained. By then I had caught Nancy's enthusiasm and was ready to try marbling for myself. In an effort to appear generous, I half-heartedly encouraged Nancy to take the class without me. She politely refused. Later we visited University of Washington's library, which houses one of the country's finest decorative book arts collections. As we pored over rare books about marbling, and admired the lovely pattern samples, Don Guyot walked in with a visitor from France. He was surprised to see us there, and with an exclamation of "All right, all right!," consented to let us both take his class.

The first day of class arrived. We went to our trays. I dropped color on the thickened water, watched the droplets expand into circles, made a pattern on the fluid surface, laid down a sheet of paper, and lifted the paper. I couldn't believe it: the floating pattern was on the paper, and it didn't wash off. My heart was racing and I was hooked! The next thing I knew, another student was at my tank lifting my leftover paint onto strips of paper. We didn't want to waste any of it. It was so beautiful.

While driving back to North Carolina, Nancy and I brainstormed a business called Indigo Stone: Indigo, for the first color that Don always used in marbling, and Stone, representing the circles of color that are first dispersed in a tank to start a pattern. I quit my job a year after my first class, and have been marbling full-time ever since. Nancy now teaches marbling and other paper arts, too. I continue to be captivated by the versatility of the amazing printing process. Whether I'm making playful refrigerator art with children, recreational prints with friends, or refined designs as a professional, every print is one-of-a-kind, and every one is magic to me.

Marbling has an intriguing history worth investigating. There is an excellent bibliography available on the Internet (see Resources, page 80). For this book, however, I'm taking my cue from my former students. When starting out, they like to skip the history and get to the good part: they just want to try marbling.

In this book, we'll review the tools and equipment you need to start marbling, introduce color theory to help you develop a palette and use paints effectively, and explore three basic marbling patterns, plus many variations. You'll learn to make your own tools with simple, inexpensive materials, and to identify and troubleshoot problems with your marbling results. The project section of the book introduces additional patterns and techniques, and presents you with lots of options for showing off your marbled papers and fabrics, from creating cards and magnets made with marbled paper to making a table runner using marbled fabrics and simple sewing. You can use the patterns and colors suggested for each project, or make up your own combinations. Finally, the gallery will introduce you to some exciting ways that artists from a variety of media have used marbled materials in their work. Most importantly, I hope the book will inspire you to ask "What would happen if...?"

Marbling is an experience not to be missed. Let it cast its spell on you.

Getting Started

Transforming drops of paint into beautiful printed patterns may seem intimidating, but it's a lot easier than you might think. You can master the basics quickly and easily, then start experimenting with colors and patterns to bring your own creative flair to any project.

MARBLING IS ESSENTIALLY AN EIGHT-STEP PROCESS:

1 Making the bath or size (a viscose solution of water and an organic gum or binder)

2 Placing the bath in an appropriate container

3 Treating your paper, fabric, or wood with alum, a mordant

4 Mixing your paint

5 Dropping the paint on the surface of the bath so that it will float and expand into concentric circles of color

6 Manipulating the paint in a fanciful pattern or image

7 Laying the treated material in the bath so the pattern transfers from the liquid to the treated material

8 Rinsing off the printed creation and drying it

TOOLS, SUPPLIES, AND MATERIALS

A basic setup with simple tools and materials is all you need to begin marbling. With a little resourcefulness, you'll be able to adapt or make everything you need from items found at home, the hardware store, or an arts or crafts store. As your involvement with marbling increases, you might want to invest in additional equipment, which can be found through sources on the Internet (see Resources, page 80). You might also want to make your own, as described on pages 10-11.

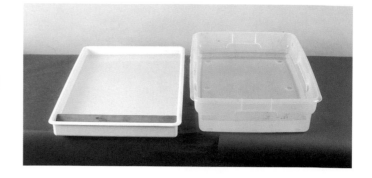

Work Space

Setting up an efficient work space will increase your enjoyment as you begin to explore marbling. Whether you're working in your kitchen, garage, basement, or studio, adapt the setup to fit comfortably in your space.

If possible, you should have two flat surfaces (such as counters or tabletops) available when marbling. One surface will hold the wet stuff, such as a tray, tools, paint, and a rinse tank. The other will hold the dry stuff, such as paper, fabric, and newspaper. You'll need a water source nearby and an area for drying your prints. Note: If you work outside, stay out of direct sunlight.

Tray and Rinsing Equipment

The tray, also called a tank, is a waterproof container with enough depth and surface area for making prints. It may be an aluminum cookie sheet, plastic storage container, plastic-lined box, photo-development tray, handmade wooden tray, or even a bathtub. For marbling paper and fabric, a 1 to 3-inch-deep (2.5 to 7.6 cm) tray is sufficient. The tray should be approximately 2 inches (5.1 cm) longer and wider than the material onto which you're printing. When marbling a three-dimensional object, the tank must be deeper than the height of the object and have enough surface area to cover its sides.

To marble paper, you'll need a rinse board (a little larger than the paper) and a plastic storage container, water and a large cup, or a sink and a hose. To marble fabric, you'll need a rinse bucket or plastic storage container.

Latex or Rubber Gloves

Keep a supply of disposable latex or rubber gloves on hand when marbling. This will save you time in clean up and protect you hands from the chemicals you'll have to mix during your preparations.

Color Applicators

You can use a variety of tools to disperse paint on the surface of the bath. As the paint droplets hit the surface of the liquid, they should expand into disks of color.

EYEDROPPER

This is one of the easiest color applicators to use when you start marbling. Use an eyedropper to disperse larger droplets of color, which will expand on the surface of the tray. Glass eyedroppers are easier to clean than plastic ones.

From left to right: Atomizer, synthetic and natural bristle whisks, brushes, eyedroppers

BRUSH

A 1 to 2-inch-wide (2.5 to 5.1 cm) round or flat brush is easy to find and good for making a small to medium Stone pattern.

WHISK

A whisk is a 1 to 2-inch-wide (2.5 to 5.1 cm) bundle of broom straw held together at one end with thin cord or a rubber band. You can easily make a whisk with the natural or synthetic fibers of a broom. The whisk is used to make a small to medium Stone pattern.

ATOMIZER

An atomizer—a small, breath-powered airbrush—uses the forced exhalation of your breath to create a mini-Stone pattern (see page 18).

Pattern-Making Tools

You can use a variety of tools to create intricate and bold patterns. A beginning set of pattern-making tools should include a stylus, two rakes (the length and width of your tray), and a comb. As you progress with marbling, you may want to make additional tools.

STYLUS

A stylus has a long point like a thin bamboo skewer and is used to manipulate colors. You can also use a chopstick, knitting needle, or even a wooden dowel as a stylus. If you start with just one marbling tool, pick the stylus. It is still my favorite.

RAKE

A rake has several narrow-to-medium-size teeth that are generally spaced 1 to 3 inches (2.5 to 7.6 cm) apart. This tool is used to elongate paint circles into straight or curved lines.

HAIR PICK

A plastic hair pick works well if its teeth aren't too thick. For the best effect, barely submerge the tips of the teeth as you pull it through the floating paint.

COMB

A comb has narrow teeth spaced $\frac{1}{8}$ to 1 inch (3 mm to 2.5 cm) apart. Again, you can easily make your own combs.

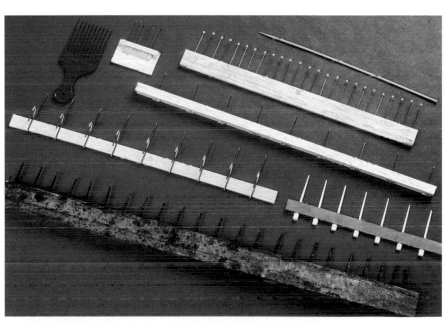

Drying Equipment

An old-fashioned collapsible wooden drying rack works for a small space. You can also set up a clothesline. Conserve space on the line by using coat hangers and clothespins. PVC drying racks are easy to make and can be cut to any size for small and large spaces (see page 11).

Newspaper

Newspaper "erasers" are used to clean the surface of the bath between prints. Strips of newspaper approximately 4 inches (10.2 cm) wide (torn with the grain of the newspaper) work well. Full sheets of newspaper are used to remove a whole pattern and start over.

Making Your Own Tools

You don't need to invest a lot of money in equipment and tools to begin marbling. You can make most of the tools you'll need in a few simple steps with common, inexpensive materials following these instructions.

RAKES

Make a rake for the length and width of the tray with teeth 1 to 3 inches (2.5 to 7.6 cm) apart. To make a handle, cut a piece of ½-inch-thick (1.3 cm) balsa wood or polystyrene foam 1 to 2 inches (2.5 to 5.1 cm) shorter than the inside measurement of the tray. Example: Make a mark every 2 inches (5.1 cm) down the center of the handle and push a T-pin through each mark.

Rake Variations

Cut a length of door screen molding and push drapery hooks over the narrow edge of the molding at marked intervals. Cut off the protruding hook with wire cutters if you wish. As an alternative, cut a piece of corrugated cardboard to fit your tray, and insert hair curler picks at designated intervals. Seal it with non-water soluble glue.

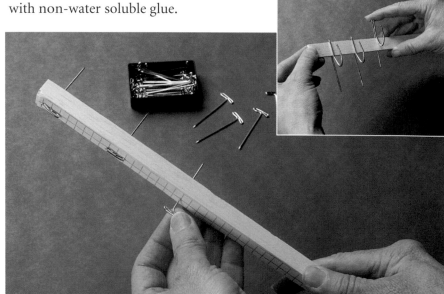

Above: Making a rake with T-pins; upper right: Making a rake with drapery hooks

WHISK

Using a common household broom made of natural or synthetic fibers, cut off equal lengths of straw, each approximately 8 inches (20.3 cm) long. Make a small bundle of straw and hold it together with a rubber band or string.

COMBS

Cut a ¼-inch-thick (6 mm) piece of balsa wood equal to your tray in width. Tape a strip of graph paper with a ¼-inch (6 mm) grid to the top. Push long dressmaker or quilt pins through the balsa every ¼ to ½ inches (6 mm to 1.3 cm). Glue the strip to a ¼ x 2-inch (6 mm x 5.1 cm) piece of balsa wood.

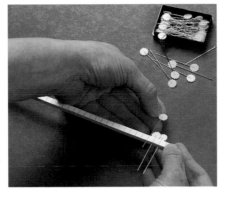

Comb Variation

Although exposed pinpoints are easier to clean, you may prefer not to prick yourself. To create an alternative handle, use a ¼ x 2-inch (6 mm x 5.1 cm) strip of balsa wood or foam core. Push each pinpoint into the narrow side, evenly spaced along the length of the strip. Secure the pins with waterproof glue.

PVC PIPE DRYING RACK

You can make a drying rack for your prints from ¾-inch (1.9 cm) PVC pipes, elbows, and plumbing fittings. PVC is easy to cut with small PVC rachet pliers. To catch drips, lay a plastic drop cloth under the rack and secure it in place with pipe insulation. Hang prints from the top of the rack by laying wooden door screen molding across the top and attach clothespins to the print. As an alternative, cut a piece of PVC pipe the length of the rack, and attach clothespins to use as handles. Drape your fabric over it.

Preparing Materials for Printing

ALUM

Alum is a solution that allows paint to bond to the fibers of paper, fabric, or wood. Aluminum sulfate and potassium aluminum sulfate are the base materials of alum, and come in a powder or fine crystal form. Alum can be found where dyeing supplies are sold, or ordered from a pharmacy (more expensive).

BATH

The bath is the liquid onto which paint is applied in a marbling tank. There are two substances generally used to create bath. The first is carrageenan, a powder processed from a seaweed commonly called Irish Moss. The second is methyl cellulose, a cellulose-based binder. When buying from a marbling supplier, ask which bath they recommend using with their paints, and find out if a product instruction sheet will be provided.

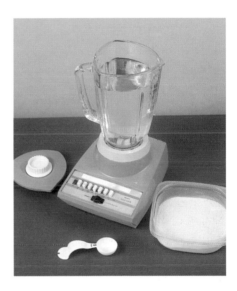

CARRAGEENAN

Processed (pre-cooked and powdered) carrageenan is easy to mix, allows crisp line quality in patterns, and rinses off easily. Carrageenan will lose its viscosity (thickness) after a few days. A shallow tank that holds an 11 x 17-inch (27.9 x 43.2 cm) piece of paper will hold about 2 gallons (7.5 L) of carrageenan bath.

Mixing Carrageenan

Because different water sources affect the viscosity of the solution, you may want to use distilled water. As a starting point, add 4 cups (946.3 mL) of water to a 1-quart (946.3 mL) blender and turn it on. While agitating, add 1 tablespoon (15 g) of processed carrageenan. Blend for 1 minute. Pour the thickened solution into a container and repeat the process with 1 tablespoon (15 g) of carrageenan. Add an additional 2 quarts (1.8 L) of water to the 2 quarts (1.8 L) of the thick solution, and let it set overnight before using.

METHYL CELLULOSE

Methyl cellulose, or methocel, is easy to mix, lasts a long time, and doesn't contaminate easily. However, it doesn't produce as crisp a line as carrageenan, and it's a little harder to rinse off. Ask your supplier for a recipe. Make enough bath to fill your container 1 to 2 inches deep (2.5 to 5.1 cm). A tank that holds ¼ yard (22.86 cm) of fabric will hold 2 to 3 gallons (7.5 to 11.3 L) of bath. Note: Methyl cellulose was used for the marbling in this book.

Mixing Methyl Cellulose

There are several ways to mix methyl cellulose. A common recipe uses pure household ammonia (no non-ionic surfactants, alcohol, perfume, or detergent) and white vinegar. Gradually add 4 tablespoons (100 g) of methyl cellulose powder to 1 gallon (3.78 L) cold water, stirring constantly until the particles are dispersed (no lumps). Add 2 teaspoons (9.8 mL) ammonia and stir until thick, like syrup. Add 2 teaspoons (9.8 mL) vinegar. Let it set a minimum of 3 hours.

One methocel recipe uses water only. Place 4 tablespoons (100 g) of methocel powder in a 2-quart (1.8 L) container. Add 4 cups (946.4 mL) of boiling water and stir until there are no lumps. Add 4 cups (946.4 mL) of ice water and continue to stir until thick. Allow the mixture to return to room temperature. Note: If you have hard water, you may need to alter the recipe. Add 2 teaspoons (9.8 mL) of blue fabric softener to 1 gallon (3.78 L) of water. Add 4 tablespoons (100 g) of methyl cellulose and 2 teaspoons (9.8 mL) ammonia (no vinegar).

CELLULOSE WALLPAPER PASTE

Cellulose wallpaper paste can be found in hardware and paint stores. Mix 2 tablespoons (50 g) of powder in 1 gallon (3.78 L) of cold water and stir until thick. If necessary, add 1 to 2 tablespoons (25 to 50 g) more for a syrupy consistency. Let it set for a minimum of 3 hours before using. It produces a fuzzier line on your prints, but may be easier to find.

PAPER

You can start marbling with a range of papers, from manila art paper to handmade mulberry paper. Manila art paper is good for practice since it's porous, doesn't need to be treated with alum, and is very inexpensive. Keep in mind though that it's acidic, and will become brittle with time. Photocopy paper is a good paper for beginner marblers because it's easy to find, inexpensive, and comes in many colors. Other papers, whether they're text weight (stationery weight) or cover weight (card stock), will have to be tested to see if they produce a clean print after being treated with alum (see Troubleshooting on pages 26-27).

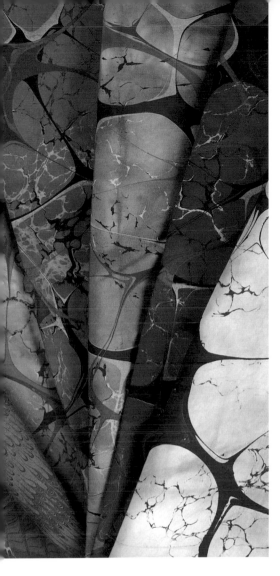

FABRIC

You can use many kinds of fabric for marbling, from lamé to upholstery. Fabrics like wools, silk noil, and sueded fabrics don't print well, and are not recommended. Cottons and blends should be washed with detergent in hot water at least once before marbling to remove sizing. Muslin produces inconsistent results. When possible, use PFD (prepared for dyeing) fabrics. Silks should be soaked in detergent water and rinsed. Upholstery fabric or canvas should not be washed.

OTHER MATERIALS

You can also marble three-dimensional objects, or objects made from wood, clay, or natural fibers.

Treating Materials with Alum

Before marbling, treat your printing surface (paper, fabric, wood, etc.) with alum so the paint floating on the bath will stick to the surface fibers upon contact. It's a good idea to have a supply of pre-treated materials on hand before you begin marbling. Wear rubber or latex gloves when working with alum.

PAPER

To treat paper with alum, dissolve 1 tablespoon (14.7 mL) of alum in 1 cup (236 mL) of warm water. Pencil an X mark on the back of your paper. Lay the paper face up on a pressboard. Fold a damp sponge in half and barely dip the folded edge in the alum solution. To treat the surface evenly, sponge the sides of the paper, then re-dip the sponge and dampsponge the whole paper with an up-and-down, back-and-forth motion. Repeat this process for up to ten pieces of paper and place a pressboard on top of the stack. Cover the stack with a heavy weight for at least 1 hour before marbling.

FABRIC

Dissolve ½ cup (118.2 mL) alum in 1 gallon (3.78 L) of warm water. Wearing latex or rubber gloves, place the fabric in the solution until it's completely wet. Gently squeeze out excess alum solution and hang the fabric to dry on a clothesline or drying rack.

Remove deep wrinkles with an iron set to medium heat. Don't scorch the fabric—extreme heat plus alum equals sulfuric acid. Note: If fabric treated with alum isn't used for marbling within a week, the alum should be washed out.

To avoid wrinkling upholstery fabric or canvas, lay it in a flat container of alum or spray it on with a spray bottle and let it drip dry. Don't wrinkle heavy fabrics. It's very difficult to remove wrinkles later.

THREE-DIMENSIONAL OBJECTS

You can apply alum to three-dimensional objects with a sponge. For wood and clay, use 1½ teaspoons (7.3 mL) to 1 cup (236 mL) water.

Preparing Paints for Marbling

ACRYLIC PAINTS

Acrylic paints vary from brand to brand in spreading properties and pigment concentration. With a couple of modifications, most acrylics will give satisfactory results. Starting out, select a brand that offers a fabric medium. Keep it on hand in case your paints won't spread when dropped on the bath. The medium will act as a surfactant, altering the surface tension of the paint on the bath. If possible, choose paint in a squeeze bottle, or in a tub that has a creamy or fluid consistency.

RECIPE

Mix 1 teaspoon (4.9 mL) of paint to 1 teaspoon (4.9 mL) distilled water in a small container. If the consistency is very thin at first, your paint may be prediluted. If you're using airbrush colors, you may be able to stretch them by adding 1 part paint to 1 part distilled water. If you're printing on fabric, or if your paints sink when dropped on the bath, add ½ to 1 teaspoon (2.4 to 4.9 mL) of fabric medium to the paint and water solution.

COLOR BASICS

Mixing a range of colors is almost as fascinating as the marbling itself. For years I have used the sensory approach to mixing colors: a little of this and my heart beats faster; a little of that, and I wrinkle my nose in displeasure. Yet, as a teacher, I have found mixing colors to be the activity that intimidates most students. This section of the book will help demystify the process.

Understanding some basic information about color will allow you to become familiar with the vocabulary of color, as well as increase your confidence to explore various combinations.

There are three characteristics of color: hue, chroma, and value.

Hue describes an actual color: red, orange, yellow, green, blue, or violet.

Chroma describes a color's intensity, its comparative brightness or dullness.

Value refers to the light or dark property of a color as it relates to white and black. A yellow hue is lighter in value than a violet hue. Value can also

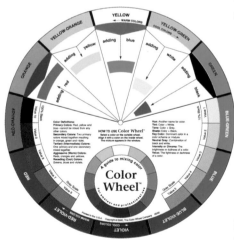

The Color Wheel Company
Philomath, Oregon

refer to the percentage of white mixed with a color to make a tint or the percentage of black mixed with a color to make a shade.

Note: Adding white will tint a color. Adding black will shade a color. Both will dull the chroma of the modified color.

The Color Wheel and Manufactured Paints

Since many people have learned about color theory through the color wheel, I will use it as a guide.

Theory: Primary colors of red, yellow, and blue are the basic colors from which all other colors are derived. Secondary colors, such as orange, green, and violet, are mixed from primary colors. Tertiary colors are made by combining a primary and a secondary color.

Reality: There are no true primary colors in manufactured paints. Paint choices usually tend to be more like tertiary colors: red-violet, red-orange, etc.

Acrylic paints are made from paint particles suspended in a polymer emulsion. Manufactured paints are made with two different

Mixing a Range of Analogous and Complementary Colors

Analogous colors are similar colors. On the color wheel (see photo on page 14), these colors are located adjacent to each other. When analogous colors are mixed together, they create a more intense color. Complementary colors are located opposite each other on the color wheel. When complementary colors are mixed together, they will neutralize one another, reducing the brightness of each color, and eventually making a neutral gray or brown. When choosing colors for marbling, you'll want to use both analogous and complementary colors to achieve the most striking results. This exercise will show you how to start experimenting with color, using the "primary" colors that you buy from manufacturers as a base to create a range of colors. By adding small amounts of each primary to the other, you'll discover the effect each color has on the other.

kinds of pigments: organic and inorganic. Paints made with organic pigments have high chroma, good tinting strength, and a transparent quality, like stained glass. Paints made with inorganic pigments have lower chroma, lower tinting strength, and tend to be more opaque. The color swatches below demonstrate the difference between the two kinds of paint.

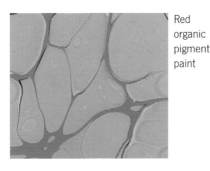

Red organic pigment paint

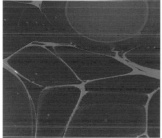

Red inorganic pigment paint

YOU WILL NEED

Red paint* (violet shade and orange shade)

Yellow paint* (orange shade and green shade)

Blue paint* (green shade and violet shade)

Black paint

White paint

Eyedropper

Brush

Measuring implements

Small containers

You need two shades of each primary color: For example, red that tends towards magenta (red-violet) and one that tends towards orange (red-orange), etc.

For Analogous Colors:

1 In separate containers, mix 2 tablespoons (29 mL) paint of each color with 2 tablespoons (29 mL) distilled water. Rinse your

eyedropper and brush for each new color. Note: Some inexpensive craft paints are prediluted.

2 Line up your paint containers, and place three empty containers between the red (violet shade) and blue (violet-shade). Place 4 teaspoons (19.5 mL) of red in the first two containers. Put 4 teaspoons (19.5 mL) of blue in the other container.

3 With a clean eyedropper, gradually add a small amount of blue to the red in the first container, stirring as you go, until a bright red-violet is mixed.

4 Wash out your dropper and gradually add enough blue to the second middle container to get

orange. Add a smaller amount of red to the third container to get a yellow-orange.

5 Use the same procedure to mix an analogous range of colors between yellow to blue (green shade) then to blue to red.

For Complementary Colors:

Use the colors you mixed for the analogous range.

1 Place three containers between the red and green that you mixed. Measure 3 teaspoons (14.7 mL) of red into the first and second containers. Place 3 teaspoons (14.7 mL) of green into the third container.

2 With a clean dropper, gradually add green to the first container, stirring as you go, until the red is darkened and subdued. Wash the dropper between color changes. Combine green in suitable proportion with red so the mixture turns neutral gray. Subdue the green with red.

3 Repeat the procedure to create a yellow to violet range.

4 Finally, mix an orange to a blue range.

MARBLING PATTERNS: SEQUENCE AND MANIPULATIONS

Once the work space has been set up, the materials have been treated, and the paints mixed, the best of the adventure begins—creating images and lifting prints.

You will discover endless design variations in marbling as you combine and explore different elements: the placement of paints, the size of patterns, the sequence of tool use, and the extent of manipulations.

The rake or comb's thickness will affect the drag, or pull, as it moves through the bath: the greater the diameter, the more drag. Generally it's best to have thinner teeth for combs in which the spacing between the teeth is narrow. It's useful to have at least one rake with thicker teeth (such as plastic picks or nails) in order to pull extended lines of color.

Marbled patterns and designs used in this book will be based on three fundamental patterns: Stone, Gel Git, and Nonpareil. We'll explore variations of each pattern.

The Stone Pattern

The Stone pattern is the baseline for all other patterns we'll see in this book. The concentric circles of color that form on the bath as droplets of paint are called stones.

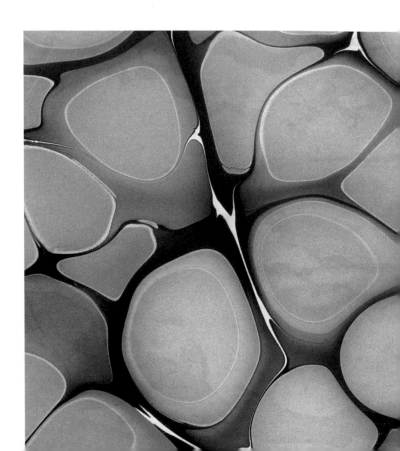

Creating the Stone Pattern

1 Skim the surface of the bath with a 4-inch-wide (10.2 cm) strip of newspaper to clean it; this will remove previously used paint and an invisible film that can disrupt the paint's ability to spread on the surface of the bath. If some remaining paint is pushed under the surface as you clean, don't worry. You're primarily concerned with the surface of the tray.

Test each color to make sure it will spread. Add 2 to 3 drops of paint. If the drops expand into circles, they're ready. If they sink, add a little surfactant, (a surface-active ingredient used to help paints float) to them. If you can't find a manufactured surfactant, you can substitute rubbing alcohol or diluted dish-washing liquid. Once the paints are adjusted and float on the water, you are ready to begin.

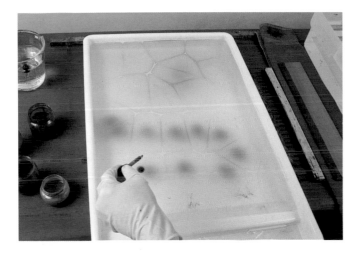

2 With an eyedropper, randomly disperse droplets of your first color (ground color) over the surface of the bath. Allow the color to spread into large circles with even saturation of color (no dark circles) before adding a second color.

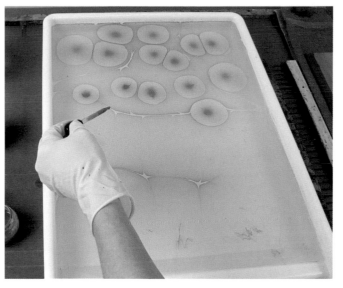

3 Add a second color. You'll observe that as the second color disperses, the first color begins compressing into veins without mixing with the second—the magic of varied surface tension.

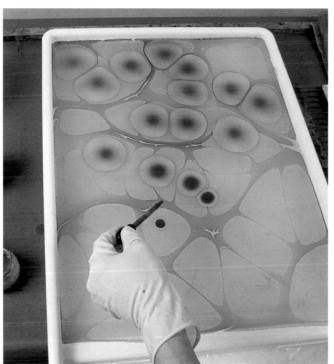

4 Add a third color in the same way.

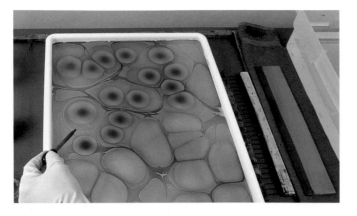

5 If you wish to add more colors, apply fewer drops of each color so as not to further compress the "ground vein." If the paint sinks instead of spreading, see Troubleshooting on pages 26-27.

8 Rinse the bath off the print in a container of water or sink, and hang it to dry.

6 Hold your paper by diagonal corners, alum side down, and lower it onto the surface of the bath.

Mini-Stone

To create a mini-Stone pattern to lightly accent another design, use an atomizer to disperse random droplets over the surface of the bath.

Open the atomizer in an L shape and place the narrower end in a small jar that contains paint at least 1 inch (2.5 cm) deep. Hold the opposite end steady and point the hinged corner of the atomizer over the base of the tray. Blow forcefully through the mouthpiece. Note: Use a plastic dropcloth to cover any area you don't want sprayed.

7 Lift the print onto a rinse board.

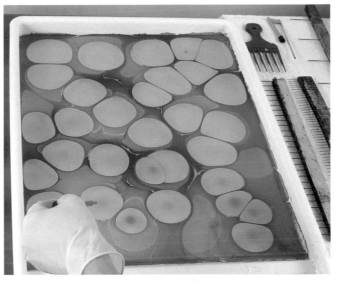

Small to Medium Stone

A small to medium Stone pattern is made with a whisk or brush. Dip the whisk or brush into your paint (an alternative is to apply paint with a dropper). Hold the whisk parallel to the surface of the bath, 12 inches (30.5 cm) away, and lightly tap it across the bridge of the index finger of your opposite hand while simultaneously zigzagging over the tray.

Note: Try dropping three to four compatible colors on a large whisk and distributing the mixture over the tray.

Large and Extra-Large Stone

A random large and extra-large Stone pattern is made with an eyedropper (as described in step 1 on page 17).

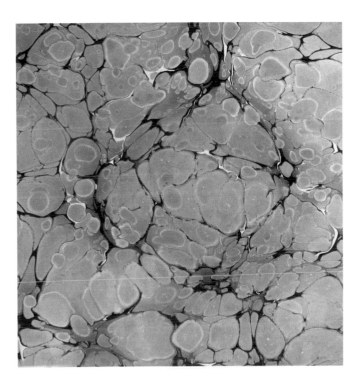

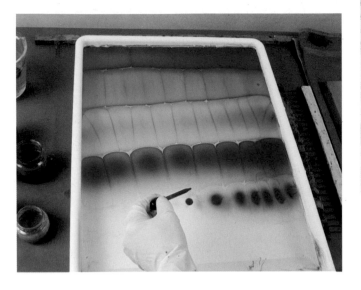

LINES

Control the placement of color on the surface of the bath by carefully applying individual drops of one color in a line formation. With a different color, add a second line of paint drops 1 to 2 inches (2.5 to 5.1 cm) below the first. Continue adding lines down the length of the tank.

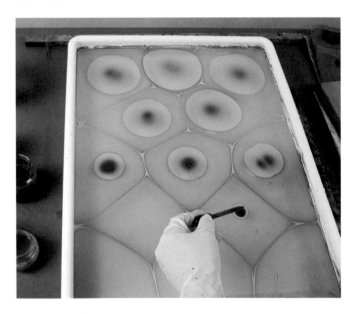

BULL'S-EYES

Bull's-eyes are made by laying drops of color 3 to 4 inches (7.6 to 10.2 cm) apart. Once the ground color has completely expanded, add a second color in the center of each expanded circle. Continue with three to five colors to create a bull's-eye effect.

Gel Git

Gel Git is Turkish for "go and come," which aptly describes the motion of the stylus or rake used to create this pattern: an up-and-down-back-and-forth manipulation. The motion pulls the Stone pattern out of a circular shape and into lines of color. The completed Gel Git pattern forms interlocking Vs of color, like the chevron patterns that adorn ancient beads or pottery.

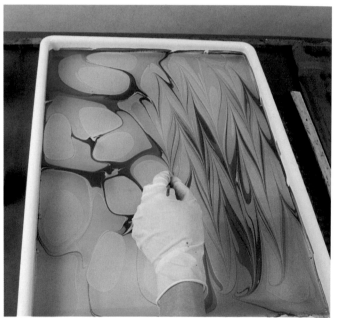

Creating the Gel Git Pattern

1 Clean the surface of the tank and lay your paints as described in step 1 of the Stone pattern. Place the end of your stylus in a lower corner of the tray and move it parallel to the length of the tray, top to bottom to top, with a zigzagging motion. Continue with this motion until you have completely passed through the Stone pattern, at which point you've made half the Gel Git pattern. This pattern is an appealing and popular pattern in itself.

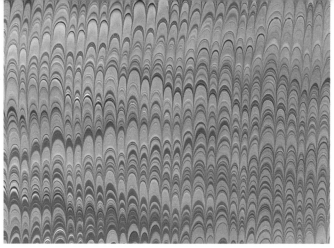

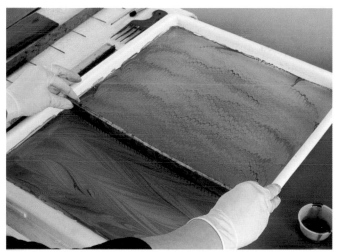

2 To complete the Gel Git, place the stylus in an upper corner of the tray and move the stylus from side to side width-wise as it progresses back and forth down the length of the tray.

GEL GIT WITH A RAKE

To create Gel Git using a rake, make a straight pass from the top to the bottom of your tank. This manipulation will create lines. Position the teeth of your rake halfway between the lines and push the rake back to the top of the tank. Repeat the process going across the width of the tank, as seen in the photo above.

Nonpareil

Nonpareil means "without equal," and seems to be the pattern that is most identified with marbling. It was, and frequently still is, used for the endpapers of books, and is often seen as a design element in many products.

Creating the Nonpareil Pattern

1 Follow all the steps for Gel Git. Using a comb with teeth ¼ to ½ inch (3 mm to 1.3 cm) apart, place the comb about halfway below the surface of the bath, and slowly pull it toward the base of the tray to make a featherlike pattern. The comb must move perpendicular to the direction from the last pull of the Gel Git.

If the Gel Git pattern moves across the width of the tank, the comb should be pulled from the top to the bottom of the tank.

VARIATIONS FOR STONE, GEL GIT, OR NONPAREIL

See the chart and illustrated patterns on pages 22–25, and the projects on pages 28–69 to learn variations that can be used to alter any of the basic patterns using a rake, comb, or a stylus.

PATTERN CHART

You've learned how to create the three basic marbling patterns, Stone, Gel Git, and Nonpareil. The following charts will help you to take your marbling a step further by showing you how to manipulate the basic patterns to create additional variations: Curl, Straight, Wave, Cable, and Spanish. The line drawings in the top row introduce the new pattern variations, which are created by pulling your rake or stylus in the direction indicated by the arrows. Since the Stone pattern is the basis for all other marbling patterns, you'll always start with a Stone pattern or one of its variations

Stone Pattern

1. Random Stone: Randomly disperse droplets of paint on the tank.

2. Lines: Drop your paint in lines across the tank.

3. Bull's Eyes: Drop a series of paint colors in concentric circles across the width and length of the tank.

Curl Pattern

Using a stylus or rake, make rows of curls by moving your tool in small spirals across the width and length of the tank.

Straight Pattern

Pull the rake from the top to the bottom of the tank in a straight pass.

Random Stone

Curl Over Random Stone

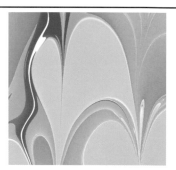

Straight Over Random Stone

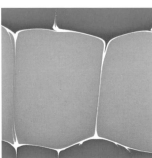

Lines

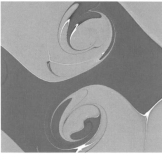

Curl Over Lines

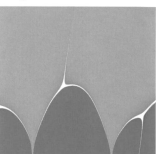

Straight Over Lines

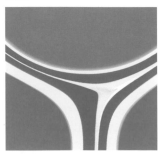

Bull's Eyes

Curl Over Bull's Eyes

Straight Over Bull's Eyes

before starting one of the additional variations. As the color chips illustrate, each pattern will have a different look depending on the Stone pattern you use to start (Random Stone, Lines, and Bull's Eyes).

In addition to illustrating pattern variations, the charts also demonstrate the results of the color mixing exercise on pages 15-16. The Stone, Lines, and Bull's Eyes chart below demonstrates the

analogous color mixing exercise. The Gel Git and Nonpareil chart (pages 24-25) demonstrates the complementary color mixing exercise.

Wave Pattern	Cable Pattern	Spanish Pattern

Wave Pattern — Pull the rake from the top to the bottom of the tank in a side to side pattern, making a wave.

Cable Pattern — Pull the rake from the top to the bottom tank in a straight pass. Shift the rake ½ inch (1.3 cm) over from the previous pass, and push it back to the top of the tank. Repeat this process until the pattern is complete across the entire tank.

Spanish Pattern — Note: The arrows indicate the direction to shift your paper, not your tool.

Hold your paper by diagonal corners. Lower one corner onto the tank and shift the paper back and forth as you simultaneously lower the opposite corner.

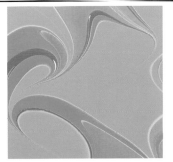

Wave Over Random Stone

Cable Over Random Stone

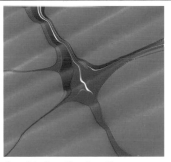

Spanish Over Random Stone

Wave Over Lines

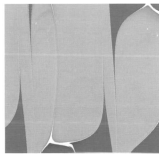

Cable Over Lines

Spanish Over Lines

Wave Over Bull's Eyes

Cable Over Bull's Eyes

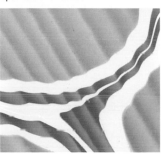

Spanish Over Bull's Eyes

On the following pages we'll see how the Gel Git and Nonpareil pattern appear when manipulated in the Curl, Straight, Wave, Cable, and Spanish patterns. Remember, the starting point for Gel Git is Stone, and the starting point for Nonpareil is the Gel Git or half Gel Git pattern.

Gel Git made from Stone

Pass through your Stone pattern with your stylus, first zigzagging up and down the tank, then back and forth across the width of your tank.
(see pages 20-21)

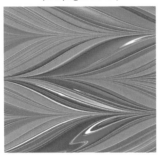

Gel Git

Curl Pattern)

Using a stylus or rake, make rows of curls by moving your tool in small spirals across the width and length of the tank.

Curl Over Gel Git

Straight Pattern

Moving perpendicular to the last pull of your Gel Git, pull the rake from the top to the bottom of the tank in a straight pass.

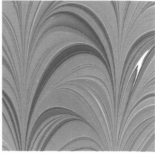

Straight Over Gel Git

Nonpareil made from Gel Git

Pull your comb from the top to the bottom of the tank, perpendicular to the last pull of your Gel Git (see page 21).

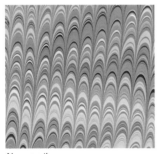

Nonpareil

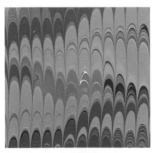

Nonpareil from half Gel Git

Curl Pattern

Using a stylus or rake, make rows of curls by moving your tool in small spirals across the width and length of the tank.

Curl Over Nonpareil

Curl Over Nonpareil

Straight Pattern

Moving perpendicular to the last pull of your Nonpareil, pull your rake across the width of the tank.

Straight Over Nonpareil

Straight Over Nonpareil

Wave Pattern

Moving perpendicular to the last pull of your Gel Git, pull the rake from the top to the bottom of the tank in a side to side pattern, making a wave.

Wave Over Nonpareil

Cable Pattern

Moving perpendicular to the last pull of your Gel Git, pull the rake from the top to the bottom tank in a straight pass. Shift the rake ½ inch (1.3 cm) over from the previous pass, and push it back to the top of the tank. Repeat this process until the pattern is complete across the entire tank.

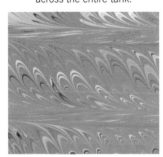

Cable Over Nonpareil

Spanish Pattern

Note: The arrows indicate the direction to shift your paper, not your tool.

Hold your paper by diagonal corners. Lower one corner onto the tank and shift the paper back and forth as you simultaneously lower the opposite corner.

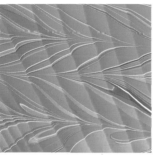

Spanish Over Nonpareil

Wave Pattern

Moving perpendicular to the last pull of your Nonpareil, pull the rake across the width of the tank in a side to side pattern, making a wave.

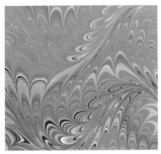

Wave Over Nonpareil

Wave Over Nonpareil

Cable Pattern

Moving perpendicular to the last pull of your Nonpareil, pull the rake across the tank in a straight pass. Shift the rake ½ inch (1.3 cm) over from the previous pass, and push it back across the width the tank. Repeat this process until the pattern is complete across the entire tank.

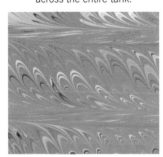

Cable Over Nonpareil

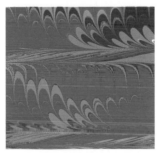

Cable Over Nonpareil

Spanish Pattern

Note: The arrows indicate the direction to shift your paper, not your tool.

Hold your paper by diagonal corners. Lower one corner onto the tank and shift the paper back and forth as you simultaneously lower the opposite corner.

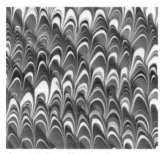

Spanish Over Nonpareil

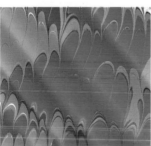

Spanish Over Nonpareil

TROUBLESHOOTING

Problem: Sinking Colors on the Bath

EXPLANATIONS AND SOLUTIONS

• The surface may be dirty. Skim the surface of the bath before applying the paint.

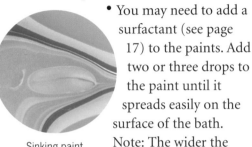

Sinking paint

• You may need to add a surfactant (see page 17) to the paints. Add two or three drops to the paint until it spreads easily on the surface of the bath. Note: The wider the paint spreads, the lighter the color will appear in the print.

• The methyl cellulose may be too thick. Add more water to the bath.

• If there are too many drops in one place, or you squeeze a dropper too hard, the surface tension may be broken. Squeeze lightly and space drops appropriately.

• If drops of color are not completely expanded before adding additional colors, the paints may sink. Be patient.

Problem: Ragged Voids

EXPLANATIONS AND SOLUTIONS

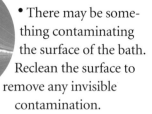

Ragged void

• There may be something contaminating the surface of the bath. Reclean the surface to remove any invisible contamination.

• Too much surfactant may have collected on the bath's surface. Again, this can be solved by recleaning the surface.

Problem: Wide-Spreading Colors

EXPLANATIONS AND SOLUTIONS

• Some colors in each brand of paint tend to spread more widely or strongly than other colors of the same brand. Identify which colors are causing the problem, and use fewer of those colors. To adjust the weaker-spreading colors to match the expansion power of the stronger spreaders, add surfactant solution or mix strong and weak spreaders together. When laying paint, use the stronger spreaders last.

• As an alternative, drop a weak surfactant solution on the bath before adding colors.

• The methyl cellulose bath may be too thin. Make a smaller amount of concentrated methyl cellulose, and add the desired amount to the thin bath. To achieve the best results, wait 2 to 3 hours before using it.

Problem: Fuzzy Edges

EXPLANATIONS AND SOLUTIONS

• The temperature of the bath may not be the same as the paint mixture.

• The bath may be too thick.

• Your paint may be too thick,

and may need to be diluted.

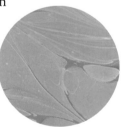

Fuzzy edges

• The methyl cellulose may not have aged long enough (minimum 3 hours, maximum 24 hours).

• The first color may not have expanded completely before you added the next color.

Problem: Paint Particles

EXPLANATIONS AND SOLUTIONS

Dry flakes of acrylic paint

• The paint may not be properly mixed. If small flakes of acrylic appear in the print, the paint may need to be re-stirred and placed in a clean container, or the dropper may need to be cleaned.

Problem: Colors Wash Off

EXPLANATIONS AND SOLUTIONS

• In paper, there may be buffers present that neutralize the alum or other additives which repel the paint.

• The alum solution may be too weak, resulting in a pale, uneven print.

• The alum solution may be too strong.

Colors washing off

Print fade out

In this case, the paint will adhere to the alum and wash or flake off in the rinse.
• The veins of the ground color may be too compressed.

• The paint may have been applied too heavily and the alum can't hold it.
• The paper or fabric may be too damp.
• The alum may not have been evenly applied to the printing surface.

Problem: Streaks, Blank Spots, White Lines, or Bubbles in the Print

EXPLANATIONS AND SOLUTIONS

Hesitation line

• A white "hesitation line" on a print results if paper is shifted while being laid on the surface of the tank, or if the paper is not laid in a continuous motion.
• Tiny spaces that appear on a print may be the result of bubbles that remain in bath after it has been poured and hasn't settled yet. Small to medium circles on a print may be caused by surface bubbles created by applying paints to the bath with a nearly-empty eyedropper, striking the

Circles on a print

Air bubbles

surface of the bath too hard with a whisk, or moving a tool through the bath too quickly. Large gaps may be created by air trapped between the bath's surface and the printing surface. Check your surface for bubbles before laying your printing material.

• The teeth of your comb or rake may be dirty. Clean your tools regularly to avoid blank spots.

Problem: Paint Breaks into Beads or Unexpected Patterns

EXPLANATIONS AND SOLUTIONS

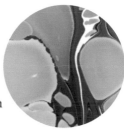

Colors breaking up on the surface

• The paint may have remained on the bath for too long and the pattern may look like a batik relief. Work quickly to avoid this problem.

Problem: Alum Problems and Dangers

EXPLANATIONS AND SOLUTIONS

• An alum solution is good for 2 months; if it's older, it may no longer be effective. If crystals form on the side of a bucket of alum, heating the solution will dissolve the crystals. If the solution has particles in it, strain it before use.

• Alum combined with high heat makes sulfuric acid. Line-dry fabric that has been treated with alum, and remove deep wrinkles with an iron on medium heat.

• Don't store fabric that's been treated with alum for more than 2 weeks as alum can weaken the fabric's fibers over time.

Other Variables

WATER

• Use distilled water to mix paints. Methyl cellulose bath made with tap water may not be compatible with the paint. Try a test batch before printing on the material of your choice.
• The depth of the bath affects the way the paints spread.
• The size of the tank affects the surface area. A small tank has more surface tension; a larger tank has less. These factors will affect the way the paint spreads.

Spanish Pattern on Fabric

Spanish is an instant favorite with anyone who tries it. The pattern creates the illusion of a third dimension on a flat surface, similar to ripples of water or the folds in fabric. The music you play while laying the material on the surface of the bath will affect the rhythm of your movements and influence the outcome of your pattern. An easy way to marble fabric is to bond the fabric to a piece of adhesive shelf paper. By backing the fabric, you can handle it just as you would handle paper.

COLOR SEQUENCE:
Green, yellow, pink, turquoise

YOU WILL NEED

Pre-treated fabric

Adhesive shelf paper

Scissors

Standard marbling supplies

Standard marbling tools

1 Cut a piece of adhesive shelf paper to fit the size of your fabric. Remove the paper backing and lay it adhesive side up on your work surface. Roll the fabric into a tube. Starting at one edge of the width, unroll the fabric onto the shelf paper, adhering the two pieces together. Cut any excess shelf paper at the edge of the fabric.

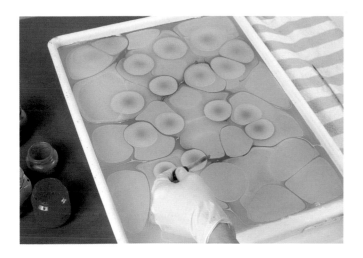

2 Lay your paints on the bath, adding as many colors as you choose.

3 Manipulate your paints with a stylus, moving with a back and forth motion in a diagonal across the tank.

4 As you are lowering your fabric on the bath, gently shift the fabric forward and back, simultaneously lowering it onto the surface of the bath.

5 Remove your fabric from the bath and rinse.

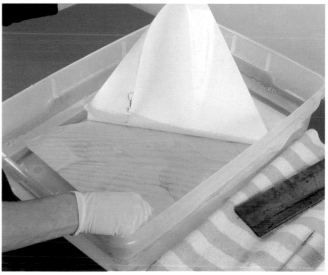

6 Remove the adhesive shelf paper from the back of the fabric and hang them both to dry. When dry, you can reuse the shelf paper to marble another piece of fabric. Once the fabric is dry, <u>iron it on the side that isn't printed to heat set the print.</u>

Note: You can achieve interesting results by lifting and lowering the paper in quarter turns as it's shifted on the bath.

Spanish Moiré on Paper

Spanish Moiré is a beautiful variation with undulating lines that create a draping effect. Folding your paper into a grid in advance is the key to creating the Spanish Moiré pattern.

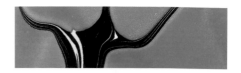

COLOR SEQUENCE:
Black, deep blue

PATTERN:
Random Stone, applied with an eyedropper

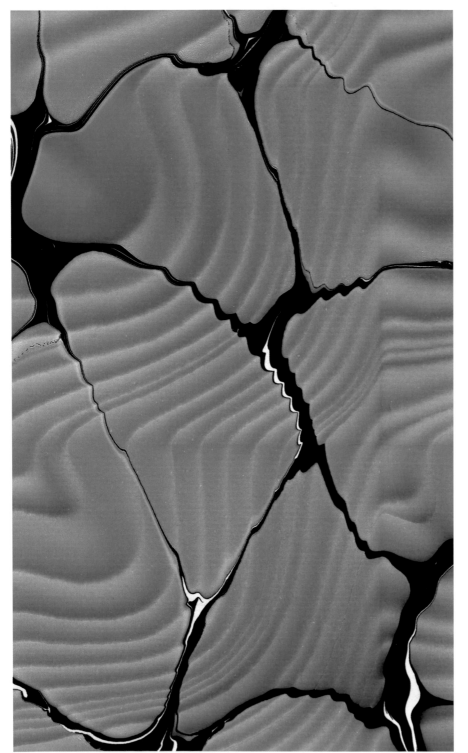

1 Lay your paper or fabric alum-treated side down and lightly fold it in 3-inch (7.6 cm) sections length-wise.

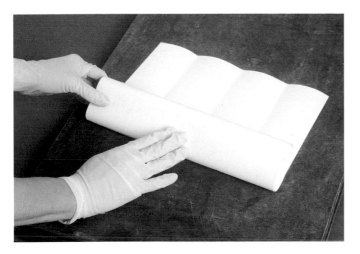

2 Unfold the paper and fold it in 3-inch (7.6 cm) sections width-wise.

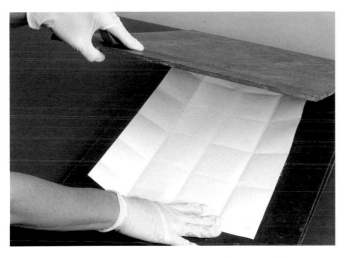

3 Unfold the paper flat again and lay it under a pressboard until ready to print.

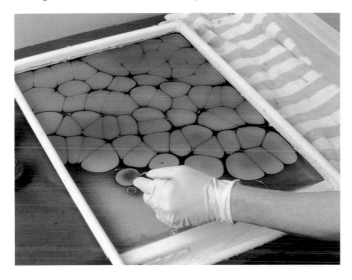

4 Lay your paints.

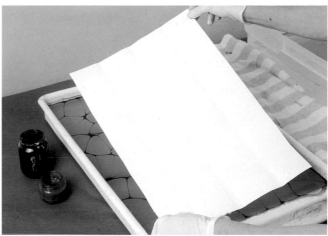

5 To create undulating lines, shift the paper forward and back as it's slowly lowered.

6 Rinse your print as usual.

Print on Print

Now that you've gotten the hang of marbling on a plain piece of paper or fabric, start layering your effects. Marble a piece of material that is printed with a pattern, such as checks, stripes, or a minifloral pattern. Choose a marbling pattern that enhances the print— big, bold marbled patterns (such as a large Stone pattern or half Gel Git) are good choices. Black and white print papers or fabrics deliver dramatic results. Attaching wooden dowels to your fabric as handles is another technique for holding your fabric while marbling.

COLOR SEQUENCE:
Dark green, lime green, orange, coral, pink

PATTERN:
Random Stone applied with an eyedropper

YOU WILL NEED
Printed fabric
2 small wooden dowels, ¼ inch (6 mm) in diameter
Pliers or wire cutters
Quliting pins
Hot glue gun and glue sticks
Duct tape (optional)
Iron
Standard marbling supplies
Standard marbling tools
Ironing board

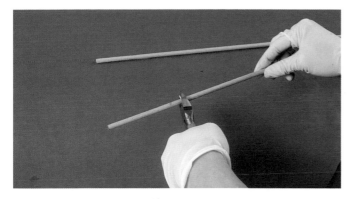

1 Cut your dowels to fit the length or width of your fabric.

2 Cut the heads off of four quilting pins.

3 Apply hot glue to the end of each dowel and attach a pin to each end, leaving a ¼-inch (6 mm) section of the pin extending beyond the edge of the dowel.

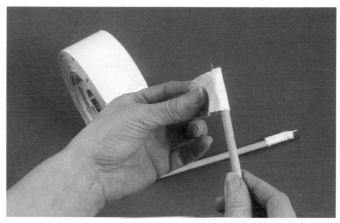

4 Once the glue has dried, apply duct tape for extra reinforcement.

5 Attach the fabric to the dowels by sticking the extended point of each pin through the fabric. Lay your paints and lower your printed fabric, printed side down, onto the bath.

6 Rinse your print and remove the dowels to use again for another project. Once dry, iron the fabric on the back side to heat set the print.

Overmarbling on Fabric

Overmarbling, or phantom marbling, describes the process of marbling a piece of material that has already been marbled. It's a lovely way to create the illusion of depth, as well as produce an interplay of design and color. It's also a great way to rescue paper or fabric that you've pronounced "ugly." Choose colors to complement the first marbled pattern you used. Since the paints used have a transparent quality, the overlapping color will mask the original print and create different tones. Coordinate your patterns, framing smaller defined patterns with a bold second print.

COLOR SEQUENCE:
First print: Green, pink, coral;
Second print: Black, green, pink, coral

PATTERNS:
First print: Half Gel Git;
Second print: Random Stone applied with an eyedropper

YOU WILL NEED

Marbled fabric

2 wooden dowels

Iron

Ironing Board

Standard marbling supplies

Standard marbling tools

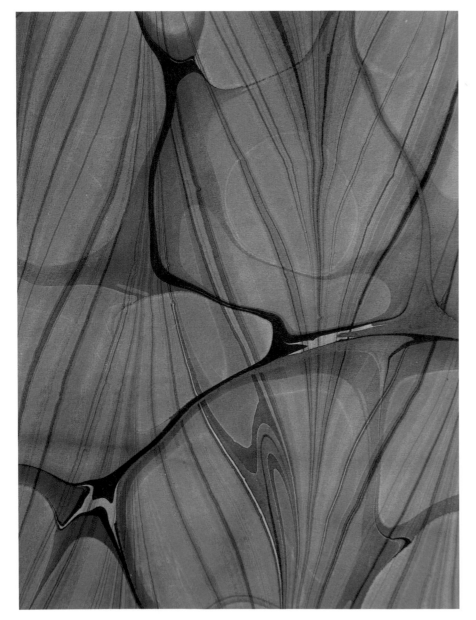

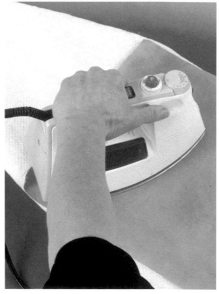

1 After creating your first print, heat set the fabric with an iron.

2 Retreat your fabric with alum, then let it dry before overmarbling.

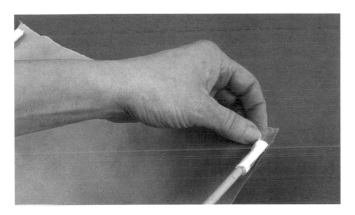

5 Lower your fabric, marbled side down, onto the surface of the bath.

3 Attach wooden dowel handles to the back side of your fabric for handling (see pages 32-33 for instructions on making handles from wooden dowels).

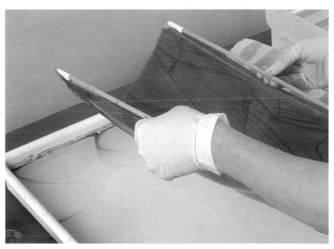

6 Lifting the fabric by the dowels, remove the fabric from the bath.

4 Lay your paints. A random Stone distribution works well for overmarbling.

7 Rinse your print as usual and remove the dowels from the fabric. Let the fabric soak in water for 1 to 2 hours to remove any bath residue left in the fabric. Hang it to dry and heat set the print.

Marbling on a Textured Surface

You can get wonderful results by marbling on jacquards, seersucker, upholstery, or handwoven fabrics (such as cotton, silk, or linen) and even synthetic lamé (anything worth doing is worth overdoing!). This jacquard-striped upholstery fabric was a handsome background for a sophisticated, feathery pattern. If you have a project in mind, experiment with a small amount of fabric first to make sure you can achieve the results that you want.

COLOR SEQUENCE:
Brown, pine green, terra cotta

PATTERNS:
Stone pattern in Lines, half Gel Git, Nonpareil

YOU WILL NEED

Textured fabric

2 wooden dowels*

Diluted surfactant

Iron

Standard marbling supplies

Standard marbling tools

*see page 32-33 for instructions on attaching dowels to fabric for marbling

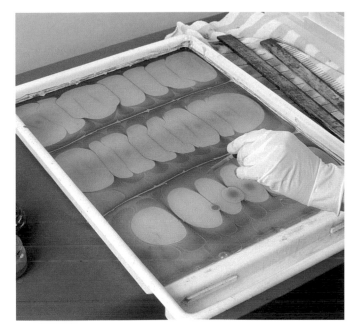

1 Lay your paints in lines.

3 Manipulate the paints with your stylus back and forth across the width of the tank to create a half Gel Git pattern.

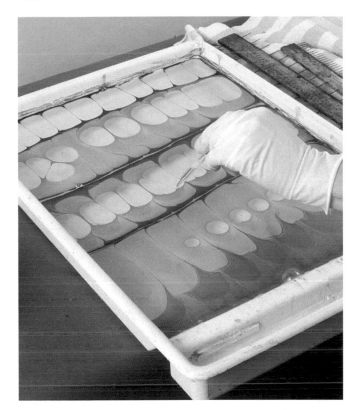

2 After laying all the colors you want, use your eyedropper to add a diluted surfactant to the bath. This will compress the color, create dramatic spacing, and allow the texture of the fabric to show clearly.

4 Drag your comb down the length of the tank to create the Nonpareil pattern.

5 Attach the dowels to your fabric. Lay your fabric on the tank, lift, rinse, and dry as usual. Heat set the print.

Lapis Lampshade

A marbled lampshade looks like a gemstone glowing from within. Creating this beautiful effect is just as easy as marbling any other surface—you only need a deeper tub. Three-dimensional objects made from wood or clay can be marbled in the same fashion. Experiment with different media, and discover the striking results you can achieve.

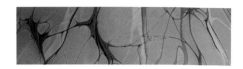

COLOR SEQUENCE:
Black, raw umber, gold, ultramarine blue

PATTERN:
Random Stone applied with a whisk, overmarbled

YOU WILL NEED

Latex or rubber gloves

Fabric or paper lampshade, 14 inches (35.6 cm) in diameter

Standard marbling supplies

Standard marbling tools

Towel

Tub, approximately 18 inches (45.7 cm) wide, 17 inches (43.2 cm) deep*

*The tub should be deeper than the height of the lampshade or object you're marbling, and have ample surface area to cover the sides of the object. The tub used here is from a farm supply store.

1 Clean the surface of the tub and apply the paint.

2 Roll up your sleeves. Turn the lampshade upside down and grasp the three-prong wire support in the top center of the shade. Gradually push the shade down through the bath.

3 Lift it out and gently rinse it. Pour alum solution over the shade once you've rinsed it, and set it on a towel to dry.

4 Clean the old pattern off the tub with newspaper. Once again, apply paints to the tub to overmarble.

5 Dip the dry marbled lampshade in the tub again to overmarble it.

6 Set the lampshade on a towel to dry.

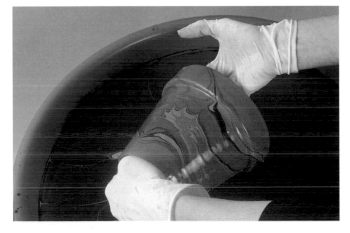

Variation

Another way to marble a three-dimensional object is to roll it over the surface of the bath. Hold the object (in this case, a flowerpot) by the rim and the hole in the base. Dip the object as you simultaneously roll it over the surface of the bath.

Gossamer Threads Silk Scarf

A marbled silk scarf always invites admiring comments. The fluid patterns of marbling are a natural complement to the fluid texture of silk. You'll need to enlist a helper for this project as it requires two sets of hands.

COLOR SEQUENCE:
Deep violet, gold ochre, taupe

PATTERN:
Random Stone applied with an eyedropper

YOU WILL NEED

Silk scarf, 8 x 54 inches (20.3 x 137 cm)

Standard marbling supplies

Standard marbling tools

Tank, 12 x 54 inches (30.5 x 137 cm)

Drying rack or clothesline

1 Clean the surface of your bath and apply your paint. This scarf uses a random Stone pattern applied with an eyedropper, but you may use any pattern you wish. Turn the scarf face down. Pick it up by two corners, and have your assistant do the same. Center the scarf over the tank, creating a slight bow in the fabric.

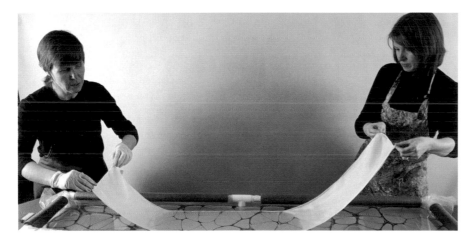

2 Lay the middle of the scarf down in the bath, then continue lowering the ends until they touch the surface. Keep a loose tension on your hold. If you pull the silk tightly, you'll create hesitation lines in the pattern.

3 When the silk appears saturated, lift the scarf from the surface by the corners and fold it in half, print side facing out.

4 One person should gather and hold all four corners of the scarf, then gently rinse it in a container or sink.

5 To dry the scarf, lay it across one or two poles on a PVC drying rack or hang it from clothespins on a hanger.

Marblescapes

Now that you've mastered the basic patterns, try creating a free-form landscape painting using marbling techniques. With a few simple strokes of your stylus, create a celestial moonscape, or a sun-filled landscape. Marblescapes make lovely framed art pieces and gifts.

COLOR SEQUENCE:
Blue, diluted surfactant

YOU WILL NEED

1 piece of 60 to 70 lb. (27.21-31.7 kg) text-weight paper

Standard marbling supplies

Stylus

Eyedropper

Skim board

1 Apply the desired colors in lines across the width of the tank: darker tones at the bottom, medium tones in the middle, and lighter tones at the top. Next, add diluted surfactant to the surface of the tank with an eyedropper.

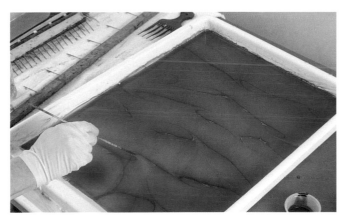

2 With a stylus, make a waved zigzag back and forth across the width of the tank from top to bottom (moving in the same direction as the lines of color).

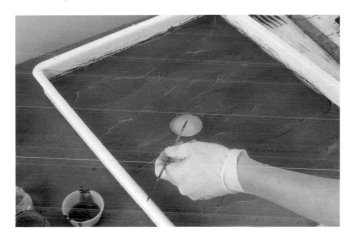

3 If you wish to make the image of a sun or full moon, place the dry tip of the stylus in paint, then touch it to the surface of the bath to form a circle.

4 Rinse your print as usual.

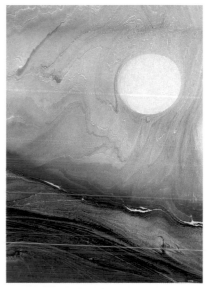

Variation

You can create a landscape, such as a hill, by pulling the paint to the bottom of your tank with a skim board and slowly pushing it back to the top of the tank.

Personal Collection Bookplate

Creating a personalized bookplate is a way to appreciate your book collection and give it the status it deserves. This attractive bookplate recalls the days when bookplates were commonly used among collectors. Follow this time-honored tradition by creating a signature marbling pattern for your own bookplates.

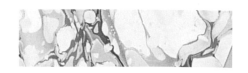

COLOR SEQUENCE:
Teal, olive, brown, ultramarine blue, pale pink

PATTERN:
Random Stone applied with a whisk

1 Brush glue on the back of the label, center it, and position it at the lower end of the 3 x 4-inch (7.6 x 10.2 cm) piece of marbled paper.

2 Brush glue on the back of the marbled paper, and center it on the 4 x 5-inch (10.2 x 12.7 cm) piece of solid-colored paper. Sandwich the paper between two pieces of wax paper, and press it with heavy books until dry.

3 Trim the solid-colored paper, leaving a ⅛-inch (3 mm) solid-colored paper border.

4 Apply glue to the back of the solid-colored paper, center it on the 4 x 5-inch (10.2 x 12.7 cm) piece of marbled paper, and press it between two pieces of wax paper until dry.

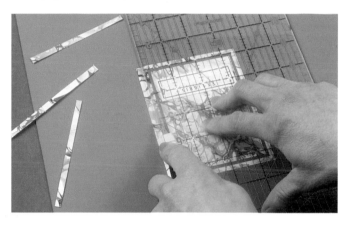

5 Trim the large piece of marbled paper that you just glued to the solid-colored paper, leaving a ⅛-inch (3 mm) marbled-paper border.

6 Apply a light layer of glue to the back of the completed bookplate, and glue it to the endpaper of your book. Lay a piece of wax paper over it before closing the cover, and press under another heavy book until dry. Once dry, the label is ready to sign.

Party Napkin Cuffs

It's the little details that make a table setting look special. These colorful napkin cuffs, inspired by origami, are just the right touch to add elegance to your dining table. Their finished appearance is so refined, you'd never know they're a snap to make.

COLOR SEQUENCE:
Gray-purple, teal, tan, light blue, violet

PATTERNS:
Random Stone applied with an eyedropper, Gel Git with Wave

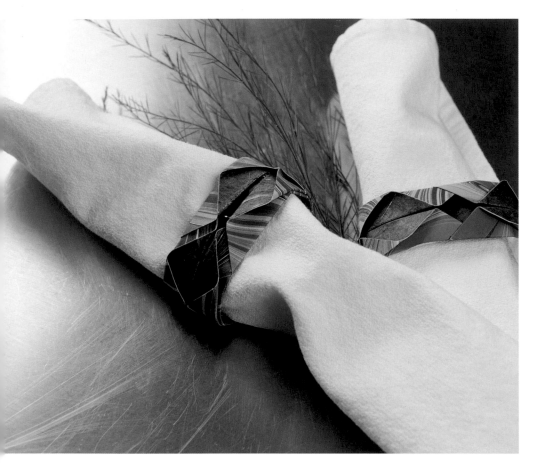

1 Glue the marbled paper to the washi paper. Press the bonded paper between two pieces of wax paper under a heavy book until dry.

2 Cut the bonded paper into 5 x 5-inch (12.7 x 12.7 cm) squares.

YOU WILL NEED

1 piece of marbled paper, 11 x 17 inches (27.9 x 43.2 cm)
1 piece of washi handmade paper (very light weight), 11 x 17 inches (27.9 x 43.2 cm)
Wax paper
Craft glue
Glue brush
Scissors
Cutting board
Clear ruler
Awl or bone folder

3 Place the ruler along diagonal corners on the washi paper side, and use the awl to lightly mark a diagonal line through the center of the square.

5 Fold the first score line toward the center of the square. Fold the second line away from the center, and continue with a fan fold to the edge of the square. Repeat the fan fold on the other half of the square.

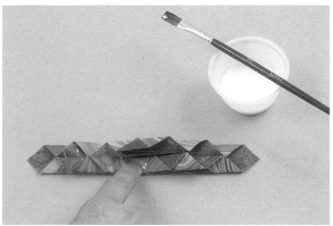

4 Lightly score another diagonal line parallel to and ½ inch (1.3 cm) from the centerline. Score another line ½ inch (1.3 cm) from and parallel to the last line you scored. Score a total of six lines in this manner until you reach the corner of the paper. Repeat the process on the other half of the square.

6 Form a pointed rectangle from the square. Collapse the folds inward, and tack the last folds together with glue.

7 Slide one pointed end inside the other to form a circle or cuff. Tack the connection with glue if desired.

Rainbow Ribbon Bookmark

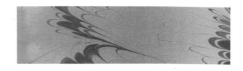

Returning to a good book that you've had to put down is always satisfying. Finding a beautiful bookmark waiting for you in your book is positively a pleasure. This bookmark is easy to make and will delight any reader. It's made from a ribbon that's pre-dyed in rainbow shades, adding an eye-catching dimension to this simple accessory.

COLOR SEQUENCE:
*Turquoise on pre-dyed ribbon
(rainbow colors)*

PATTERNS:
Stone in Lines spaced with diluted surfactant, half Gel Git, Nonpareil with Wave

YOU WILL NEED

Marbled synthetic or silk ribbon, about
2 x 9 inches (5.1 x 22.9 cm)

Adhesive bonding web for fabric*

Eyelet

Decorative cord (optional)

Iron

Scissors

Awl

Eyelet pliers

*Craft glue may be used in place of the adhesive bonding web.

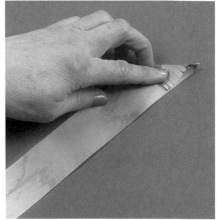

1 Lay the ribbon face down on a flat surface, and fold the top right corner flush with the opposite edge of the ribbon. Crease the ribbon, forming a triangle.

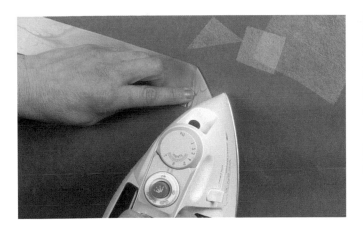

2 Cut a piece of the adhesive bonding web a little smaller than the size of the triangle. Lay the web flush against the interior fold of the triangle, and press it with an iron for 5 seconds until it fuses to the ribbon.

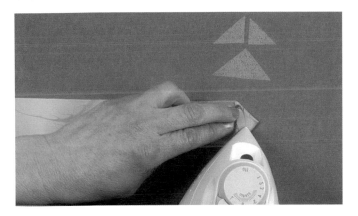

3 Fold the upper left corner of the triangle to the opposite corner. Cut a piece of adhesive bonding web to the proper size, and bond the folded corner to the triangle to create a point.

4 With an awl, punch a hole ⅜ inch (9.5 mm) from the triangle's point. Widen the hole with the eyelet pliers, and attach an eyelet.

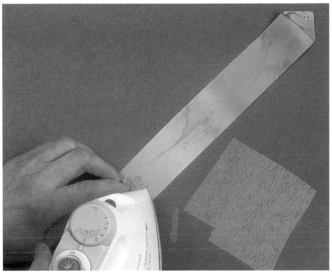

5 To create a more finished look, fold back a ¼-inch (6 mm) section of ribbon on the end opposite the triangle, and attach it in place with adhesive bonding web.

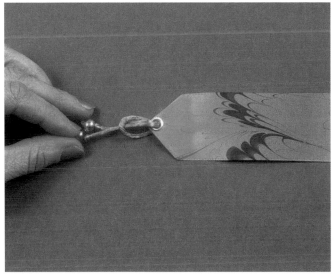

6 If desired, thread decorative cord through the eyelet hole.

Marbled Magnets

Stick notes to your fridge or bulletin board with style. These magnets, covered in marbled paper, add vibrant dashes of color to any surface and help draw your eye to important items that you don't want to forget.

COLOR SEQUENCE:
Spruce green, teal green, golden yellow, violet

PATTERNS:
Random Stone applied with an eyedropper, half Gel Git, Spanish (see pages 28-29)

YOU WILL NEED

2 squares of marbled paper (in different patterns), 3 ½ x 3 ½ inches (8.9 x 8.9 cm) and 1¾ x 1¾ inches (4.4 x 4.4 cm)

1 square of solid-colored paper, 3 x 3 inches (7.6 x 7.6 cm)

1 square of mat board, 2½ x 2½ inches (6.4 x 6.4 cm)

Peel-and-stick magnet sheet, 2 x 2 inches (5.1 x 5.1 cm)

Craft glue

Clear acrylic varnish spray

Glue brush

Craft knife

Mat knife (utility knife)

Cutting board

Clear ruler or quilter's ruler

1 Place the 3½-inch (8.9 cm) square of marbled paper face down and apply a thin layer of glue, working from the center out. Center and bond the 2½-inch (6.4 cm) square of mat board to the back of the marbled paper.

2 Bevel each corner of the marbled paper, ⅛ inch (3 mm) from each corner of the board.

3 Fold the top side of the paper over the edge of the mat board, and apply pressure to glue it in place. Repeat for the bottom side, and for the last side of the square. Sandwich the piece between two pieces of wax paper and place it under a heavy book until dry.

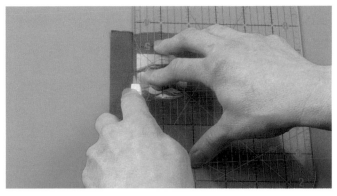

4 Apply glue to the back of the 1¾-inch (4.45 cm) marbled-paper square, and attach it to the center of the 3-inch (7.6 cm) solid-colored paper square. Lay the bonded papers on a cutting board. Trim the solid-colored paper, leaving an ⅛-inch (3 mm) solid-colored paper border.

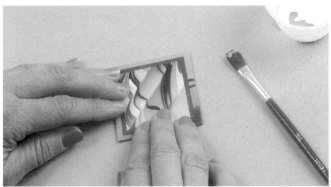

5 Turn the bonded paper face down, apply glue to the back. Center it face up on the marbled-paper covered mat board. Apply clear acrylic spray to protect the surface.

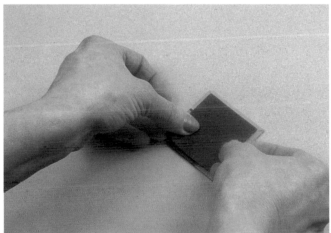

6 Peel the protective paper off the 2-inch (5.1 cm) magnet square to expose the adhesive, and attach it to the back of the marbled square.

Special Delivery Cards and Envelopes

In today's world of high-tech communication, a note or letter written on a handmade card tells the receiver you took the time to make your message personal and memorable. Marbled papers are a perfect way to embellish a handmade card or stationery. Stamped images create a layered look that is simple yet stylish.

COLOR SEQUENCE:
Teal green, gold, copper, spring green on black paper

PATTERNS:
Random Stone applied with an eyedropper, atomizer, diluted surfacant, Wave

YOU WILL NEED

Blank card and matching envelope,
5 x 7 inches (12.7 x 17.8 cm)

2 pieces of marbled paper, 2 x 7 inches
(5.1 x 17.8 cm) and 2 x 6 inches
(5.1 x 15.2 cm)

2 pieces of solid-colored paper, 3 x 7
inches (7.6 x 17.8 cm) and 3 x 3½
inches (7.6 x 8.9 cm)

1 piece of card stock, 2 x 2½ inches
(5.1 x 6.4 cm)

Craft knife

Cutting board

Synthetic sponge

Rubber stamp

Pigmented stamp pads
(pale and metallic colors)

Glue

Clear ruler or quilter's ruler

Awl

Poster tape
(double-sided tape with paper backing)

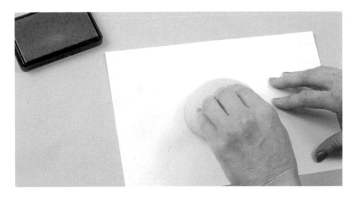

1 Cut a 2-inch (5.1 cm) circle from your synthetic sponge. Texture the surface of a blank card by pressing the sponge on a pale colored ink pad of a pale color and blotting it randomly on the card.

2 Apply glue along the back edges of the 2 x 7-inch (5.1 x 17.8 cm) piece of marbled paper. Center and bond the marbled paper to the 3 x 7-inch (7.6 x 17.8 cm) piece of solid-colored paper. Cut the solid-colored paper, leaving a ⅛-inch (3 mm) marbled-paper border.

3 With an awl, lightly score a line 1 inch (2.5 cm) in from the folded edge of the card. Apply glue to the reverse side of the bonded paper panel and position it along the scored line, flush with the top and bottom of the card. Press it firmly to the card.

4 Sponge the 2 x 2½-inch (5.1 x 6.4 cm) piece of card stock in the same manner described in step 1. Stamp an image on the card stock. Apply glue to its reverse side, center it, and bond it to the remaining piece of solid-colored paper. Cut the solid-colored paper, leaving a ⅛-inch (3 mm) border around the card stock. Apply glue to the back of the solid-colored paper, position it, and bond it to the card, as seen in the photo above.

5 Stamp your envelope. With an awl, lightly score a line on each side of the image. Attach poster tape to the back of the 2 x 6-inch (5.1 x 15.2 cm) pieces of marbled paper. Turn the marbled paper face up, and cover all but a ⅛-inch (3 mm) strip with the ruler. Cut two ⅛-inch (3 mm) strips with a craft knife. Remove the backing from the poster tape, and position each strip along the score lines, sticking them in place on the envelope. Cut the ends flush with the envelope.

Touch of Gold Fan

Brighten up that lonely corner of your mantel or side table with a touch of gold and a flourish of marbled paper. This charming fan displays your marbling talents and complements any decor. Make a large fan, and you'll have a stunning fireplace screen.

COLOR SEQUENCE:
Copper, chestnut brown, gray, brick red, gold on black paper

PATTERNS:
Gel Git, Spanish (see pages 28-29)

YOU WILL NEED

1 piece of marbled paper, 11 x 17 inches (27.9 x 43.2 cm)	Staples
1 piece of solid-colored washi paper or metallic wrapping paper, 14 x 17 inches (35.6 x 43.2 cm)	Monofilament, 6 inches (15.2 cm) long, at least 6 lb. (2.72 kg) test
1 piece of solid-colored paper, 1 x 5 inches (2.5 x 12.7 cm)	Ruler
Craft glue	Scissors
Wax paper	Glue brush
2 round doorknobs, approx. 1½ inches (3.8 cm) in diameter, each with a ½-inch-long (1.3 cm) shaft	Bone folder
	Awl
	Bolt cutter
	Stapler

1 Brush a light coat of glue on the back side of the marbled paper, center it, and bond it to the back of the solid-colored paper. Trim ½ inch (1.3 cm) off each end of the bonded paper so that it measures 16 inches (40.6 cm) long. Leave a ½-inch (1.3 cm) border of solid-colored paper along the length of the paper at the top and bottom. Apply glue to the ½-inch (1.3 cm) solid-colored border, fold it over the marbled paper, and press it in place. Repeat for remaining side. Press between two pieces of wax paper under heavy books until dry.

2 Turn the bonded paper marbled-side down, and score parallel lines along the width of the paper at 1-inch (2.5 cm) intervals. Fan fold the paper, marbled side out.

3 Compress the paper into an accordion fold, and draw a line across the center of fan.

4 Along the centerline, punch a hole ¼ inch (6 mm) in from each folded edge with an awl, making sure it punctures all the way through the layers of the fan's folds. Pass the monofilament through the holes, and tie it off with a double knot, as shown in the photo. Clip the extra line about ½ inch (1.3 cm) from the knot.

5 Cut off the head of a doorknob screw with a bolt cutter, leaving a 1-inch (2.5 cm) thread rod.

6 Screw the two doorknobs together on each side of the rod until the shafts of the doorknobs almost meet.

7 Place the attached knobs in the center of the collapsed fan, and raise the two ends of the top side of the fan. Staple the sides together along the edge.

8 Cut a 1 x 5 inch (2.5 x 12.7 cm) piece of the solid-colored paper, and fold it in half. Glue it over the stapled seam in the fan to cover the staples.

Treasure Box

Make a storage box as special as the keepsakes you put inside it. Marbled paper is a perfect solution for enhancing a plain cardboard or wooden box. Choose your favorite patterns and colors, marble your paper, and with not much more than scissors and glue, create an attractive accent piece that you'll want to display, not hide away.

COLOR SEQUENCE:
Black, turquoise

PATTERNS:
Random Stone applied with an eyedropper, Spanish Moiré (see pages 30-31)

YOU WILL NEED

Template, page 77
Pencil
Lidded cardboard or wooden box, 4 x 6 x 3 inches (10.2 x 15.2 x 7.6)*
1 or 2 sheets marbled paper, each 11 x 17 inches (27.9 x 43.2 cm)
Ruler
Craft glue
Scissors (or cutting board and craft knife)
Glue brush

*Adapt the template to match the size of your box.

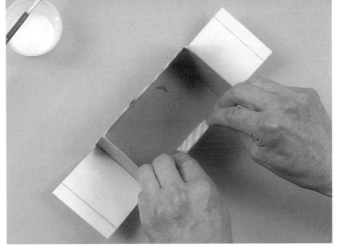

1 Using the template on page 77 as a guide, draw a pattern on the reverse side of your marbled paper. Make the appropriate cuts as indicated on the template.

3 Lay the marbled paper face down and apply glue. Lay the base of the box within the traced area, and adhere a long section of the marbled paper with winged tabs to the wall and lip of the box. Repeat on the opposite side.

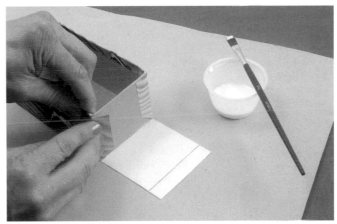

2 Crease the lines where a fold is indicated.

4 Adhere the tabs to the short side of the box on each end. Adhere the remaining sections of marbled paper to the short side and lip to finish covering the box.

5 Complete the lid by following the process described for the box.

Playful Pinwheel Ornament

*Hang it on your Christmas tree or simply dangle it from a windowsill. This pinwheel ornament
will captivate you with its swirling shape and colors. Following a simple template,
it's easy to make and lets you show off your best marbled paper designs.*

YOU WILL NEED

Pinwheel template on page 77

1 piece of marbled paper,
8½ x 11 inches (21.6 x 27.9 cm)

1 piece of solid-colored handmade
paper or foil wrapping paper, 8½ x 11
(21.6 x 27.9 cm) inches

1 piece of plain paper, 8½ x 11 inches
(21.6 x 27.9 cm)

Tracing paper

Craft glue

Wax paper

1 headpin (jewelry finding), 2 inches
(5.1 cm) long

2 beads (sized to fit the headpin)

1 piece of monofilament, 6 inches
(15.2 cm) long

½-inch (1.3 cm) paste brush

Scissors or craft knife

Awl

Needle-nose pliers or round-nose
jeweler's pliers

Wire cutters

COLOR SEQUENCE:
*Ultramarine blue, golden yellow,
teal green, brick red*

PATTERNS:
*Random Stone applied with an eyedropper,
half Gel Git, Spanish (see pages 28-29)*

1 Glue the handmade or foil wrapping paper to the marbled paper. Cut the bonded paper into 4 x 4-inch (10.2 x 10.2 cm) squares. Cut a plain sheet of paper into a square of the same size to use as a template. Using tracing paper, copy the template on page 77 onto the plain white paper. Place the copied template on top of the bonded square, and create holes by punching through both with an awl at the appropriate marks with an awl. Copy the X shape from the template onto the bonded paper.

2 Cut along the X mark from the end of one arm to the punched hole near the center. Repeat for the other arms of the X.

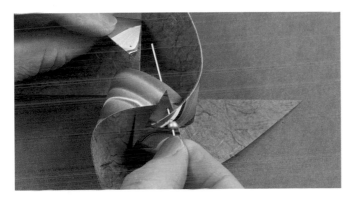

3 Slide a bead onto the headpin, and push it through the hole near the end of each arm of the pinwheel.

4 Pass the headpin through the center hole. Add one more bead. Cut about ¾ inch (1.9 cm) off the stem of the headpin.

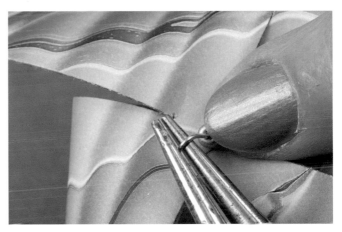

5 Use the pliers to form a small circle on the open end of the headpin, and form a closure.

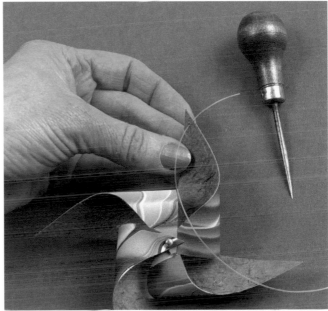

6 Punch a hole near the end of one of the X arms. Thread a piece of monofilament through the hole and tie a loop.

Vine Dance Table Runner

A splendid table setting can make any meal feel like a special event. This marbled fabric table runner is the perfect accent piece for your buffet table or sideboard. Choose complementary colors and patterns for your fabrics, and experiment with big, bold marbled patterns on contrasting backgrounds, such as checked or floral fabric. You don't need advanced sewing skills to make this project— just a sewing machine and a few simple seams.

COLOR SEQUENCE:
Spruce green, overmarbled with sage green and khaki

PATTERNS:
Random Stone applied with a whisk, and a pattern I call "vine dance" (Bull's eyes followed by diluted surfactant, manipulated randomly with a stylus)

YOU WILL NEED

6 pieces of marbled cotton-checked fabric, each 2 x 13 inches (5.1 x 33 cm)

2 pieces of marbled cotton minifloral fabric, each 3 x 13 inches (7.6 x 33 cm)

3 pieces of marbled cotton-checked fabric, each 6 x 13 inches (30.5 x 33 cm)

1 piece of solid-colored cotton marbled fabric, 6 x 13 inches (15.2 x 33 cm)

2 pieces of solid-colored cotton marbled fabric, each 22 x 13 inches (55.9 x 33 cm)

1 piece of cotton minifloral fabric (not marbled), 13 x 72 inches (33 x 182 cm)

Straight pins

Spool of thread

Needle

Iron

Long ruler

Scissors

Bone folder

Sewing machine

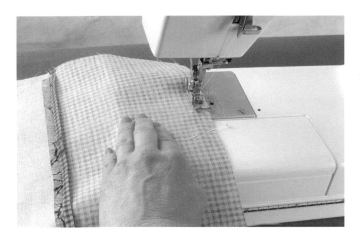

1 Using ¼-inch (6 mm) seams, sew the fabric panels together across the 13-inch (33 cm) width, alternating the panel patterns to create the design of your choice. I suggest using the solid-background 6 x 13-inch (15.2 x 33 cm) marbled piece in the center. The completed panel is approximately 6 feet (1.8 m) long. The long minifloral piece, which is not marbled, will be the lining. Iron the seams open.

2 Lay the right side of the panel you created in step1 face to face with the right side of the 13 x 72-inch (33 x 182 cm) lining. Trim the lining to match the length of the runner, and pin the two pieces together. Beginning about 2 inches (5.1 cm) from the center of the runner, sew a ¼-inch (6 mm) seam to the corner. Continue along the length, across the opposite width, and along the remaining length. End about 4 inches (10.2 cm) from where you started, leaving a 4-inch (10.2 cm) opening.

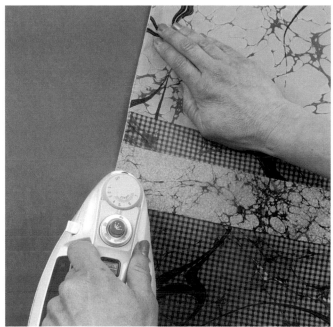

3 Remove the pins. Bevel the corners of the fabric ⅛-inch (3 mm) from the corner seam. Turn the runner right-side out through the 4-inch (10.2 cm) opening. Use a bone folder to push the four corners into points. Press the seams flat with an iron.

4 Stitch the 4-inch (10.2 cm) gap closed by hand.

Charming Gift Bag

Give gifts with extra appeal—present them in a marbled paper gift bag that is a gift in itself. Alter your marbling patterns and palettes according to the occasion your gift celebrates: red and green for Christmas, soft colors for baby and bridal showers, bold hues for birthdays. You can even dress up a plain brown paper bag with marbled paper cut into a shape, such as a pinwheel. Your friends and family will appreciate the fine packaging and will surely save the bag to use again.

COLOR SEQUENCE:
Black, violet, blue, green, red, orange, yellow

PATTERNS:
Stone in Lines, half Gel Git, Nonpareil

YOU WILL NEED

Template on page 78

1 piece of marbled paper, 11 x 17 inches (27.9 x 43.2 cm)

Pencil

Ruler

Scoring tool, such as a bone folder

Wax paper

Craft glue

Decorative cord

Glue brush

Eyelet pliers or hole punch

Eyelets

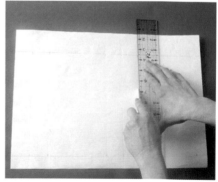

Instructions for Bag

1 Using the template on page 78 as a guide, mark corresponding lines on the back of your marbled paper. Score the lines across the width of the marbled paper, starting from the left. Then score the lines across the top and bottom length of the paper.

2 Crease your first and second vertical lines in. Crease the third line out, the fourth and fifth lines in, and the sixth line out.

3 Open out the paper and crease the horizonal lines in along the length of the paper. Apply glue along the inside edge of one hoizontal fold to reinforce the rim of the bag.

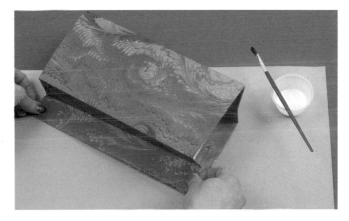

4 Refold the rest of your score lines and apply glue along the outside 1-inch (2.5 cm) vertical fold of one side of the bag. Line up the glued fold with the edge of the opposite side and bond the two together, pressing firmly in order to secure the bond.

5 To make the bag's base, lay it down with the unfinished edge facing you. Fold in the left side of the base along the scored line. Line up the scored line from the left with the scored line on the bottom and crease it at a 45° angle. Fold in the right side in the same manner. Turn the bag over. Repeat the procedure for the remaining side by folding in the left and right sides to form a flap on each side.

6 Apply glue to the inside of each flap and press together. Set the bag down on a piece of wax paper and place a heavy weight (such as a bottle of water) inside the bag until the glue has dried.

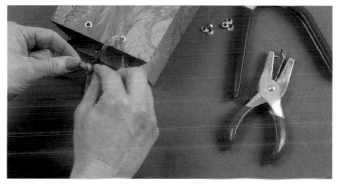

7 To add the handles, punch 2 holes near the top side of the bag, ½ inch (1.3 cm) from the top of each side of the bag. For a sturdier handle, use eyelets applied with eyelet pliers. Cut two pieces of cord to the desired length. Thread each piece through both holes on one side and knot each end on the inside of the bag. Repeat on the opposite side of the bag.

Handsome Marbled Frame

Transform an ordinary double-mat frame by covering it with a marbled paper in deep, rich colors. The trick to making a frame with a polished appearance is to bevel cut the corners and tuck in the paper, leaving no rough creased or crumpled lines. The resulting frame has a crisp, professional appearance.

YOU WILL NEED

2 pieces of marbled paper, 10 x 12 inches (25.4 x 30.5 cm) and 2 x 12 inches (5.1 x 30.5 cm)	Craft glue
	Wax paper
1 small piece of card stock	Glue brush
1 piece of mat board, 8 x 10 inches (20.3 x 25.4 cm)	Craft knife
	Cutting board
Double frame mat with an easel, 8 x 10 inches (20.3 x 25.4 cm)*	Mat knife
	Clear ruler

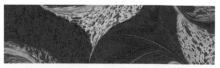

COLOR SEQUENCE:
Brick red, ochre, gold, copper on black paper

PATTERNS:
Random Stone applied with an eyedropper, atomizer, and diluted surfactant, Wave

* The color of your inner mat should complement the colors in your marbled paper.

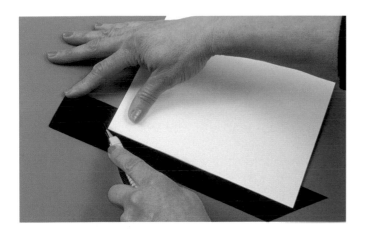

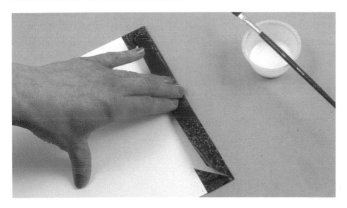

1 Apply glue to the 2 x 12-inch (5.1 x 30.5 cm) piece of marbled paper, and center it on an 8-inch (20.3 cm) side of the mat board. Bevel cut the edges of the marbled paper at a 45° angle, 1/8 inch (3 mm) from each corner of the mat board.

3 Separate the double mat, and set aside the inner mat. Lay the outer mat face up and apply glue to its entire surface. Lay the remaining piece of marbled paper face down, and center the mat board glued-side down and press in place. Mark and cut a 3 x 5-inch (7.6 x 12.7 cm) section of marbled paper from the center of the mat on the paper (glued-side down) and press. Starting at the inside corner of the mat, cut at an angle to the edge of the 3 x 5-inch (7.6 x 12.7 cm) hole.

2 The bevel cuts you made in step 1 create two triangular tabs. Fold them over each edge of the mat board. Tuck the tabs at the corners, and fold the remaining paper over the mat board. Sandwich the covered mat board between two pieces of wax paper and press with a heavy book until dry.

4 Apply glue to the inside paper border. Fold each section of paper back to cover the inside edges of the mat board window. Don't cover the outer border yet.

5 Apply glue to the back of the outer mat, and adhere it to the inner mat.

6 Turn the double mat face down. Remove a triangle of marbled paper ¼ inch (6 mm) from each corner of the double mat. Apply glue to one width of the border only, and fold it over the back of the double mat. Sandwich the double mat between two pieces of wax paper, and weigh it down with a heavy book until dry.

7 The double mat remains face down with the covered side closest to you. Lay the solid piece of mat on the double mat with the covered edge on top of the covered side of the double mat. Apply glue to the remaining three sides of the marbled paper.

8 Fold the paper opposite the covered side over all three pieces of mat board. Tuck the 1/4 inch (6 mm) paper border over two corners and fold the paper over the back. Repeat for the remaining side.

9 Apply glue to the back of the easel, and center it on the back of the frame. Sandwich the completed frame between two pieces of wax paper, and weigh it down until dry.

Tri-Fold Desk Screen

Does your desk face a blank wall or a pile of clutter? An attractive desk screen made of marbled fabric panels can improve your view and add a sophisticated flair to your work space. Marble fabrics in colors to match your decor, sew them together, and cover a simple framework made with precut parts.

COLOR SEQUENCE:
Spruce green, copper, brick red, ochre, light orange on dyed fabric, overmarbled

PATTERNS:
Random Stone applied with an eyedropper, diluted surfactant, overmarbled

*Available at craft stores

1 To make a fabric panel, pin a 6-inch-wide (15.2 cm) piece of marbled fabric to a 3-inch (7.6 cm) wide piece of solid-colored fabric. Connect the pieces with a 3/8-inch (9.5 mm) seam along the length of the fabric. Add on a 9 inch (22.8 cm) width of marbled fabric to the panel. Iron the seams open. Repeat this process for two more panels of the same sequence, and three more panels of the opposite sequence.

2 Each canvas stretcher has grooves on each end, which allows two stretcher pieces to interlock, forming a corner. Four interlocking stretchers make a framework. Assemble three canvas stretcher frameworks, each 14 x 27 inches (35.6 x 68.6 cm).

3 Lay down a panel of fabric that you've sewn together. Center the framework on the panel so that there is a 1½-inch (3.8 cm) edge of fabric on all four sides. The panel will be attached to the framework much like stretching a canvas. Beginning at the center of the top length, lay the edge of the fabric over the back of the stretcher and staple it. Pull the fabric so it's tight through the middle, and staple the opposite edge of fabric to the center of the parallel stretcher. Pull the fabric over one side stretcher, and staple it in the center, then repeat for the other side. Return to the top stretcher and continue the process by attaching the fabric about 2 inches (5.1 cm) from each side of the center staple. Repeat the sequence until the fabric is stapled to about 3 inches (7.6 cm) from each corner.

4 Tuck in the fabric at the corners as if you're wrapping a package. Secure with a staple.

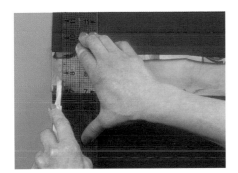

5 To cover the front of the screen, lay down a fabric panel and center it on the framework, covered-side up. Mark the outline of the framework with a pencil and remove the framework. Trim the fabric panel to 1 inch (2.5 cm) from the framework line with scissors or a craft knife.

6 Turn a ½-inch (1.3 cm) fold around the panel's edge and press it in place with an iron. Miter the corners by lifting the overlapping corner fold into a protruding triangle and clipping off the triangle with scissors.

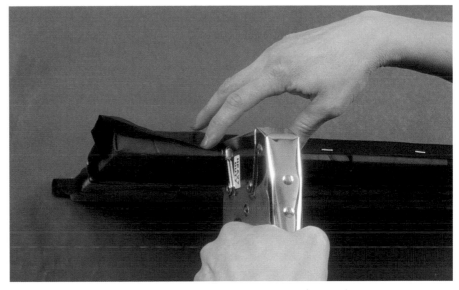

7 Re-center the framework on the panel. Beginning with the center of a long side, staple the folded edge of the fabric to the outside edge of the framework following the instructions for step 3, except in this case you're stapling the fabric to the outside edge, not the back of the framework.

8 Measure and mark 5 inches (12.7 cm) from each corner on the long side of the framework. To attach a hinge, lay the top of the hinge flange just below the mark on the framework's edge, with the hinge pin facing down. Using an awl, punch through the screw holes and insert the screws. Stand a second screen next to the first, and lay the free flange on the second section. Line up the ends, punch the mark, and insert the screws. Repeat on the other end. Turn over the two hinged sections, align the third section, and attach the hinges in the same way.

9 Apply the matching trim around the outside edges with a glue gun to give the screen a decorative finish

MARBLING GALLERY

Marbling is a collaborative medium by nature. When individuals presented in the gallery were asked to share their work, or to incorporate marbled materials into their medium directly or by inspiration, their response was enthusiastic. The result is a visual feast of ideas.

Susan Lightcap, *Untitled.* 6 x 9 inches (15.2 x 21cm). Quarter-bound books with exposed spine bands, compound binding of silk and hand marbled paper with Coptic and sewing-all-along stitches.

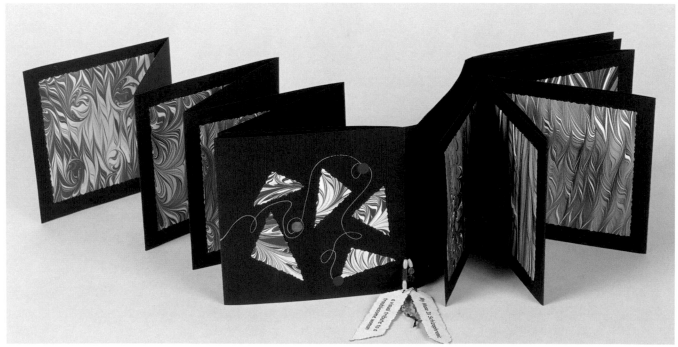

Nancy Dunn Lawrence, *My Muse Is Schizophrenic: A Visual Tribute to a Troublesome Woman.*
6⁷/₁₆ x 6½ x ⅝ inches (16.3 x 16.5 x 1.6 cm). Marbled paper, scraps, and glue.

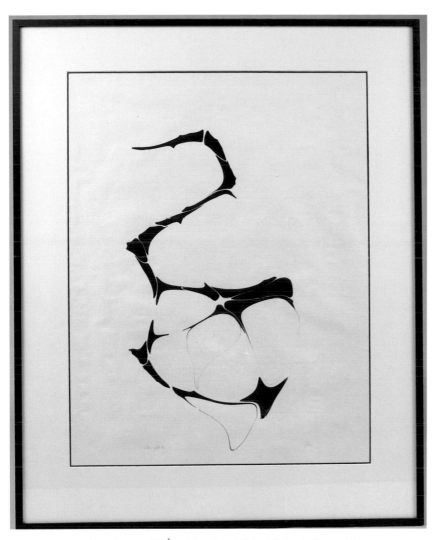

Laura Sims, *Swan's Reflection*. 23 ½ x 29 inches (59.7 x 73.7 cm). Monoprint acrylic on paper.

Mary Jane Miller (marbling by **Mimi Schleicher**), *Two Black Birds*. 18 x 40 inches (45.7 x 101.6 cm). Marbled black paper.

Mimi Schleicher, *Untitled*. 25 x 25 x 1 inches (63.5 cm x 63.5 cm x 2.5 cm). Marbled black paper.

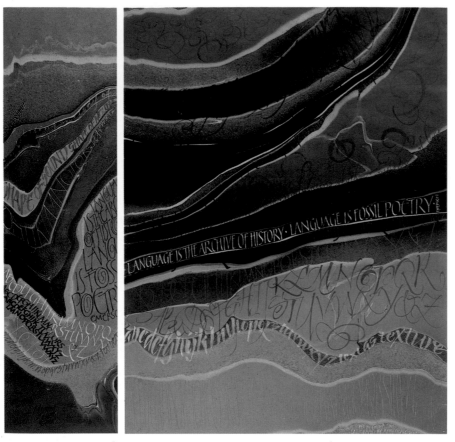

Annie Cicale, *Untitled*. 6 ⅝ inches x 22 inches (16.8 cm x 55.8 cm) and 17¼ x 23 inches (43 x 58.4 cm). Gouache on marbled paper; steel pens, and sable brushes.

José A. Fumero, *Untitled*. 16 x 14 inches (40.6 cm x 35.6 cm). Marbled paper (Laura Sims), silk, cotton, clear acrylic paint.

Rodger Jacobs, *Untitled*. 9½ x 12 inches (22.8 x 6.3 cm). Turned wood candlestick.

Kristyn Woodland and **James Currier**, *Untitled.* 4¼ x 4¼ inches (10.8 x 10.8 cm). Ceramic tiles.

Beth Kelley Zorbanos, *Untitled.* 10 inches (25.4 cm). Corn husk, raw silk, sheep's wool, raw flax.

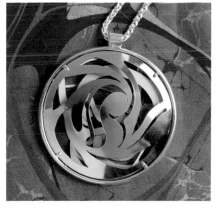

James Charneski, *Phantom Curl.* 2 inches (5 cm) wide. Sterling silver and gold plate.

Peggy Debell, *Plastic Flamingo.* 17 x 23 inches (43.2 x 58.4 cm). Digitally-altered photo, marbled fabric, hand embroidery, machine-pieced and hand-quilted photo transfers.

Patti Quinn Hill, *Pot of Gold.* 13½ x 10 inches (34.3 x 25.4 cm). Cotton, acrylic paint, archival watercolor paper, waxed linen, and handpainted birch handles.

Liz Spear, *Golden Box Top*. 30 x 16 inches (76.2 x 40.6 cm). Handwoven fabric of cotton, rayon, and cotton-blend yarns.

Laura Sims, *Evening Wrap*. 90 x 22 inches (229 x 59 cm). Silk charmeuse, velvet, glass beads.

Linda Bair, *Untitled*. 24 x 20 inches (61 x 50.8 cm). Purple silk charmeuse; beige silk duppioni trim.

Douglas Atchley, *Untitled*. 30¾ x 12¾ inches (78.1 x 32.4 cm). Blue and brown silk habotai. Arashi shibori.

Bill Cook, *Untitled* . 7 x 5 inches
(17.8 cm x 12.7 cm). Ash wood.

Dee Dee Triplett, *Coppice Moth*. 14 inches (35.6 cm) tall. Black and white rayon, linen, polysuede, silk/metallic, beads, hand-forged iron base; machine embroidered.

Edwina Bringle, *Untitled*. 16 x 13 inches (40.6 x 33 cm). Marbled canvas, machine stitch embroidery.

Joan Bazzel, Top: *Rude Ruffle*. 2⅞ x 2 inches (7.2 x 5 cm). Vitreous glass enamel on copper opaque scrolling technique; brass mesh, nickel silver, glass beads. Left: *Ojo Azul*. 2⅞ x 1¾ inches (7.2 x 4.4 cm). Brass mesh, nickel silver, and labradorite set in sterling. Right: *Fuego*. 3 x 1¾ inches (7.6 x 4.4 cm). Brass mesh, nickel silver, carnelian set in sterling.

Rachel Reese, *Myth*. 31½ x 37¼ inches. (79 x 94.2 cm). Marbled cotton fabrics, dyed cotton and poly/cotton fabrics, cotton batting, metallic and poly/cotton threads.

Annamarie Poole, *Untitled*. 62 x 66 inches. (157.5 x 167.6 cm). Cotton fabric, cotton batting.

TEMPLATES

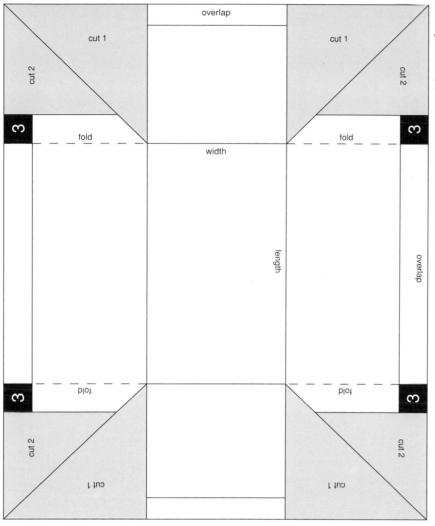

Treasure Box Template

Project pages: 56-57

**Playful Pinwheel
Ornament Template**

Project pages: 58-59

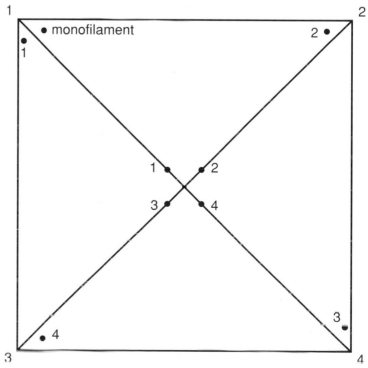

TEMPLATES

Charming Gift Bag Template   Project pages: 62-63

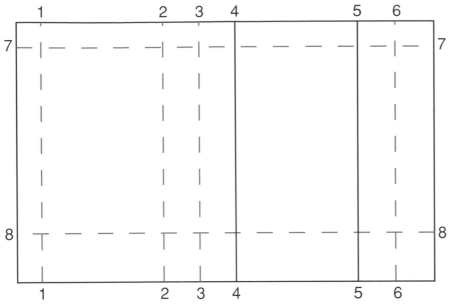

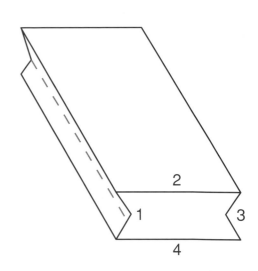

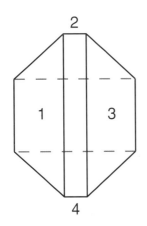

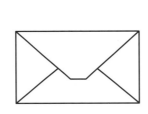

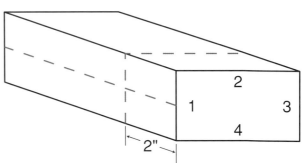

Party Napkin Cuffs Template

Project pages: 46-47

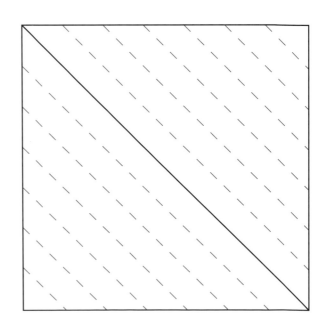